A TREE WITHOUT ROOTS

PAUL CROOKS was born a stone's throw from Wembley Football Stadium and lives in London. He started searching for his African slave ancestors after being told it was not possible. He is the author of *Ancestors* (BlackAmber), a fictionalised account of his great-great-great-grandfather's part in the struggle for emancipation from 1798 to 1838.

A TREE WITHOUT ROOTS

The Guide to Tracing British, African and Asian Caribbean Ancestry

Paul Crooks

ARCADIA BOOKS

Arcadia Books Ltd
139 Highlever Road
London W10 6PH

www.arcadiabooks.co.uk

First published by BlackAmber (an imprint of Arcadia Books) 2008
Reprinted by Arcadia Books 2014

A catalogue record for this book is available from the British Library.

ISBN 978-1-905147-81-6

Typeset in Warnock by MacGuru Ltd
Printed and bound by CPI Group (UK) Ltd, Croydon CRO 4YY

Arcadia Books supports English PEN *www.englishpen.org* and
The Book Trade Charity *http://booktradecharity.wordpress.com*

Arcadia Books distributors are as follows:

in the UK and elsewhere in Europe:
Macmillan Distribution Ltd
Brunel Road
Houndmills
Basingstoke
Hants RG21 6XS

in the USA and Canada:
Dufour Editions
PO Box 7
Chester Springs
PA 19425

in Australia/New Zealand:
NewSouth Books
University of New South Wales
Sydney NSW 2052

To Mum & Dad
To Sandra, Chenaii & Abenna
And to my brothers, nieces and nephews

The future is bright.
Look for it beyond the horizon.

Contents

Introduction

Just before my first book *Ancestors* was published in 2002, my wife asked me whether I had any reason to believe people would be interested in tracing their Caribbean ancestry. I knew what was on her mind; it was the same thing that played on mine. It had been more than twenty years since Alex Haley's seminal offering *Roots*. Had the assassination attempts made on his iconic status succeeded? Had people simply lost the enthusiasm to follow in his path? Or had apathy set in, with people convinced about the impossibility of his achievement? The silence on the research front was eerie; there were no reports of any successes or media interest whatsoever. I had mentioned in the Afterword to *Ancestors* that my wife and I had attended a talk on Caribbean family history at the Society of Genealogists. We were surprised at the low attendance by African Caribbeans. Just two families, including mine, had attended. We had observed that Black History Month was losing its *raison d'être*; its focus on African achievement down through the ages. Alex Haley's *Roots* left an indelible impression on me when it was first screened in England in 1977. So, despite the barometer readings, I was sure that *Roots* had similarly inspired many others of my generation. So, my answer to my wife's question was a simple 'yes'.

I had five aspirations when *Ancestors* was published. The first was to share all that I had discovered about my family origins with anyone that shared my passion about family. The second was to enshrine my family's history so it could be passed on to future generations. Thirdly, I hoped that *Ancestors* would encourage people of a similar cultural background to myself to take collective action to preserve their stories and those of the Windrush generation – the forebears who first came to settle in Britain after the Second World War. Fourthly, I wanted readers to see in a positive light the challenges our ancestors had to overcome to stay alive; the unspoken courage, physical and mental determination, leadership and hope that sustained them. Lastly, I hoped it would stimulate a more critical exploration of Caribbean history, especially by those among us that manifest the psychological effects of our traumatic past, and those who had been misinformed about aspects of the abolition of the slave trade.

The publication of *Ancestors* coincided with the landmark *Motherland* documentary. I felt then, as I do now, that the programme mocked the seriousness with which African Caribbeans born in the UK view the search for identity. It did, however, lay bare the possibilities of DNA testing. Scientists had discovered the means to link people with Caribbean connections to their motherlands, and ancient past. It also coincided with the National Archives' plans to make archives more accessible to 'recently' arrived minority communities in Britain: Africans, Asians, Jews and other migrant and refugee communities. I would like to acknowledge the enthusiasm and the effectiveness with which Sarah Griffiths, a Community Development Worker at the National Archives spearheaded their programme. Since 2002, there has been a surge in serious Caribbean history events and projects, and media interest in the subject. The Caribbean genealogy landscape has changed.

This book seeks to answer the questions that fell beyond the scope of the Afterword to *Ancestors*, the factual account of my quest. This book contains chapters intended for absolute beginners with intentions of finding out who they really are. Others seeking ways to overcome the barriers and pitfalls preventing them from achieving successful outcomes will, I hope, find support within these pages.

It is the case that many falter because they do not appreciate how a little bit of knowledge about the local history of the island in question goes a long way to overcoming some of the barriers. A section outlining the migration on Caribbean history should help with the contextual issues that can facilitate analysis and inter-pretation of your discoveries, and push you evermore forward.

I am profoundly grateful to Rosemarie Hudson, BlackAmber Books, who urged me to take on this project in 2003. The truth is I wasn't particularly motivated by the prospect of taking it on. I had other interests that I wanted to pursue. I wanted to move on. Yet increasingly, I had been getting requests to attend speaking engagements. Rosemarie picked up on the fact that I was getting a lot of questions that focused mainly on the research I undertook; questions partially addressed in *Ancestors*. There were questions that had not been fully dealt with in any one publication that I was aware of. But requests to attend speaking engagements kept coming. I wanted to answer the questions as fully as possible. I found that by reading as much as I could about Caribbean history, I was able to improve on responses to questions by enriching the context. The more challenging and incisive questions usually came, surprisingly, from young people – often eight- to thirteen-year-olds. Eventually, enthusiasm for the original idea of writing this guide crept up and patted me on the back.

You do not have to have a research background to get the best from this guide. If you have some family research experience, then you will gain further insight and the motivation to break through the barriers that have presented themselves thus far. It is important to know how to overcome the psychological obstacles preventing you from beginning or following through on your quest. Research-ing family history can be rewarding on many levels. Locating hard documentary evidence involves detective work.

Carefully consider how you're going to present your information. Family trees are not the be-all and end-all, but they
are great for sharing your findings. Family trees can provide an
important focus for passing on values and beliefs that ancestors
once held.

The basic requirement for achieving success is a high level of
commitment, the ability to get from one geographical location
to another, and a bit of good fortune. Start by finding out what
is involved before committing to anything serious. Find out how
much time you might expect to put in, in order to get something
out. Talking to like-minded individuals already engaged in the
process is the best way of doing this. Then ask yourself how much
time you are prepared to commit to tracing back? When you
know the answers to these questions, you will know what your
next steps are and how far you want to take them.

You will travel only as far as your motivation will propel you.
The guide begins by highlighting simple, motivational techniques
to get you started and maintain your enthusiasm. You may find
that you are unable to trace your ancestor back to the place of
origin – to the motherland. Anyone that has managed to do so
would have had the guidance of ancestors. Tracing back two or
three generations may be the best you will achieve.

Knowing where to find key sources of information, and how
to access it is explained, as well as presenting it in creative and
interesting ways. You may even come across information that you
are not sure how to interpret. The challenge to you, as a fledgling
family historian, is to develop your own skills in order to prevail
over the circumstances – and meet challenges head-on. Preparation is key to tackling any challenge life presents.

This easy-to-follow guide will help you get the best from information held in public records and make real progress towards
building a practical understanding of how to research your family
tree. Family history taught within a formal education setting can
instil a sense of self-esteem and confidence in young people. So

this guide has been written for family and professional educators in mind.

Part I – Tracing Back in Time – guides you through a process, from turning an expressed desire to find your roots to achieving a successful outcome, however you define this; from overcoming the psychological barriers preventing you from getting started, to extracting evermore accessible nuggets of information buried in public records over many decades. It is primarily written with ordinary people in mind; people inhibited by time and resources.

Part II – History Unmasking the Mystery – will help you to understand why certain avenues of inquiry are likely to be more challenging to pursue than others. When you determine the answers, you may find things that increasingly informed the dreams and aspirations of your forebears for present and future generations. Whatever you discover in public records was created for a reason. Some documents may appear to tell you little at first sight. The section describing the local history of the Caribbean is designed to help you to interpret, analyse and place the documents you uncover in some kind of historical context and timeframe

The case studies are designed to help overcome specific barriers preventing you from reaching your goals. These are based on my experiences and lines of inquiry. A case study by itself can never fully capture the richness and complexity of an individual line of inquiry. These can be so varied. Neither do they illustrate good or bad research and practice. The purpose of including them is to enlarge on specific issues and provide practical examples of how to tackle issues you may come up against; they should enable you to link theory with practice. The case studies included in this guide do however demonstrate: how the problem was initially identified; and the pathway to resolving particular issues.

Part I

TRACING BACK IN TIME

The Challenge

Out Of Many, One People

Jamaica's National Motto

There are lessons to be learned from the African held in bondage and the indentured servants who overcame adversity when they entered into contracts to labour on plantations in the Caribbean during the nineteenth century. Information about the existence of the ancestors on these same plantations and about the many people that made the one is of interest to people who value historical insight.

People who have researched their family history are equipped to interact with others from diverse backgrounds with great assurance. This has obvious benefits to sustaining a society where people are able to get along; where difference is valued. The seeds of sustainability are planted when family history is taught at an early age.

Those who understand the chain of historic events explaining how we came to occupy this time and space are well placed to determine their future. To know the past is to understand the present. To understand how you got to your present is to understand how to shape your future and lessen the impact of challenges foreseen and unforeseen.

When they came to the UK, the Windrush generation could not have appreciated the extent to which they were making history. They had pressing issues on their minds, like finding a way to make a living. They came from the Caribbean Islands and from former British colonies 'with hope in their eyes', to use the title of the book by Vivienne Francis. Our fathers and grandfathers were the catalyst for a massive change in the British political, social, economic and cultural landscape. Unlike previous generations of migrant communities to Britain, Caribbean immigrants and their children would present, by their very presence, a robust challenge to established ideas of what it means to be British.

The symbol of the Sankofa bird looking backwards, over its shoulder away from its direction of travel, is a very important symbol to the people of Ghana. Looking back symbolises one looking back to their roots. Whoever finds their roots is regarded as a warrior.

Rastafarians harboured thoughts of one day returning to Africa. As reggae artistes and icons, they heightened the consciousness of Africa as the ancestral home of black and mixed-heritage/black Caribbean people. In so doing, they created a fertile ground for exploration of the past, and an appetite for embracing ideas of identity.

Alex Haley's novel and television serialisation, *Roots*, inspired a generation to search for their family trees. *Roots* captured the imagination of African Caribbeans in Britain at a time when the youth were identifying with the struggles of Africans at home and abroad.

Family, community and national cohesion are abundant where history is a manifestly important part of structured education programmes. It is also a salient feature of progressive communities. It has been that way since the earliest civilisations. Marcus Garvey likened a people without a history to a tree without roots. A tree without roots simply withers and dies. The same danger befalls any community that becomes detached from its history. A culture cannot continue in perpetuity unless its people are in touch with the history that gave birth to it in the first place. Progressive societies maintain history in order to convey stories of the nation's struggles with itself and with outside forces that may have once tried to dominate it. The stories usually depict a conflict the nation faced at some time or other; the stories end with how the challenges faced were overcome. History often tells of such struggles, and of someone, a leader, who emerged to save the day. These leaders become iconic figures and greatness is bestowed on them. Their names are enshrined in history and they achieve national status as heroes. The stories of war are enduring. A nation's history will almost always recount its victories. Recent British history enjoys recalling Chancellor Chamberlain's ill-fated attempt to appease Hitler; when the land was thrown into a state of confusion as the Second World War ensued. Prime Minister Winston Churchill – his status sealed as saviour of the nation – became arguably the greatest Briton that ever lived.

When looking at African Caribbean history, the greatest struggle was for the freedom of Africans held in bondage on the slave plantations. This was, without doubt, a low point in African history. Yet two of the most important Caribbeans to emerge during that conflict had been Toussaint Breda L'Ouverture and Sam 'Daddy' Sharpe. Their titanic struggles would precipitate the ending of slavery and change the course of British and world history.

A close inspection of African history taught within the confines of structured British education reveals a catalogue of African diasporians who aspired to servitude as opposed to leadership. The hidden stories are of the battles won. As a consequence there can be no reference to inspirational leaders. This is natural and in keeping with the systematic process of nation-building when the interest of the majority is to maintain their confidence and belief in themselves as a great nation by repeating, sometimes embellishing, success stories. History can and is used to reinforce nationhood and feelings of superiority of one people over another. This partially explains why the stories of great Africans who stood at the helm of the struggles for justice, liberty, equality and brotherhood, are off the menu of those told to our young. The approach to using history as a tool for nation-building in Britain has had disastrous consequences for African and Caribbean youth. This systematic process of nation-building has proved a major barrier to the progression of people with a Caribbean heritage. Caribbean youth are exposed to few relevant examples of African and African Caribbean leaders at any of the key stages of their early education. This has to be a contributory factor when explaining away the dearth of quality leadership from within Caribbean communities. If you don't know where you're coming from, the chances are you don't know where you're going; and if you're going nowhere, then any road will get you there. Black Britons continue to face towards African American culture in search of strong iconic role models and leaders. Our young cloak themselves in identities that are alien and often negative. Many are unconscious of notions of who they are, where they come from and how or why it is they find themselves acting the way they do.

The challenge is to raise the confidence of our young to achieve their potential. Children need to develop an understanding of their personal histories at key stages to raise their confidence and self-esteem. This applies to all people regardless of cultural identity. Parents committed to sowing the seeds of family cohesiveness see the rationale for putting aside time to discuss the family history with their children. Family history should be an integral part of a structured learning package that encourages different children from different backgrounds to enter into open and dignified dialogue as a means of first understanding and then accepting differences.

Family history should be central to thoughts of shoring up family cohesion and rooting stability. It is a cornerstone of promoting identity and cohesion within all communities. Strong, stable, prosperous communities retain strong links with the past. They are held together by their commitment to their legacies and traditional values. They manifest independence and demonstrate high levels of self-esteem and identity. Understanding the sequence of historical events supports our understanding of how we find ourselves in the conditions we are in today. Revisiting, analysing and embracing our sometimes traumatic past helps us to impose ourselves on the key factors that affect our ability to pursue long-term happiness.

The historian in the family has a duty to encourage the next generation to engage with their past. They can do this by emphasising the positives that exist within them as a result of legacies that have been passed down through generations.

When the key attributes are understood, young people can liberate their understanding of what they should expect of themselves and their futures.

The African-American intellectual Cornel West, in his book *Race Matters*, defines nihilism in America as 'the lived experience of coping with a life of horrifying meaninglessness, hopelessness, and (most important) lovelessness'. What applies to American citizens also applies to British citizens. We are all greatly influenced by 'celebrity, comfort, convenience, machismo, femininity, violence, and sexual stimulation that bombards consumers'.[1]

We care less for service to others which was handed down by preceding generations. People living in poverty 'with a limited capacity to ward off self-contempt and self-hatred'[2] are most likely to succumb to the nihilistic threat to 'Black' Britain.

When we see what is happening around us today – cultural decay; the cold disengagement of our young (with a self-destructive disposition to the world) from others, elders and parents; and their crumbling dignified responses to adversity – we are entitled to ask ourselves the question: Is nihilism now seeded in Britain? The appalling number of homicidal assaults by young whites, Asian and black men on one another is – on the surface – the sign of an empty quest for pleasure, property and power, the lingering effect of Caribbean history[3] (predominantly European and African in origin) on the one hand. It is as much the consequence of government policy and corporate market institutions which today have an overwhelming influence on how societies are being shaped.

Courageous thoughts and actions aimed at laying foundations for a better future are impeded by historic inequalities which speak to the flaws in British society and the long-standing cultural stereotypes.[4] These have much to do with a perception of who we are in a place in society.

One such cultural stereotype – fatherlessness in Caribbean communities – undermines gallant efforts by community-spirited people with strong aspirations for building cohesive families and community networks. The negative impact on fatherlessness is most visible in comparatively poor areas of Britain – the inner cities. But then this is true for all people of all cultures living in the so-called developed world. Research has shown that fatherless families affect adults, children and society. The experience of fatherlessness suppresses the best what the next generation can become.

By understanding how our forebears in Africa and on the plantation created sustained communities we can begin to eclipse the vicious circle of family fragmentation on an unprecedented scale.

Cornel West discusses the prospects of black America. He could so easily be talking about black Britain here:

The genius of our black foremothers and forefathers was to create powerful buffers to ward off the nihilistic threat, to equip black folk with cultural armour to beat back the demons of hopelessness, meaninglessness, and lovelessness... traditions of black surviving and thriving under usually adverse new world conditions were major barriers against the nihilistic threat. These traditions consist primarily of black religious and civic institutions that sustained familial and communal network and support.[5]

Families that emphasise kinship can make a positive impact on their community. The historian in the family is well placed to promote kinship. They know how to actively encourage older members in their role as potential custodians of the past. In doing so they promote general well-being and protect the elders from the corrosive effects of isolation.

Where to Begin

Here, in the stories still told by the old
I feel the soul and heartbeat of my race
Which I cannot feel, in tales by strangers told
For here, within my heart these have no place
The tree grows well and strong, Oh children mine
It roots deep within the native earth
So, honour thy ancestral lines
And traditions of thy land of birth[6]

Identifying Your Quest?

Imagine yourself as a first-class sprinter lining up for a major race. You are called to the blocks by the starter. The race is about to begin. You're set in your blocks awaiting the sound of the gun. When you hear it, you rise out of the blocks, and in a split second you've taken your first stride. The gun sounds again after the first few strides; it is the sound of a false start – yours. You slow to a halt and return to your blocks to start all over again. The pressure is now on. You need to dispel the nerves. Otherwise you are defeated before the race has begun. You've prepared well, you are mentally strong, and that is key if you're going to get off to a good start the next time the gun sounds for the race against time.

Before you start searching, be clear about why you're pursuing your quest. Ask yourself, 'What am I looking for?' A lack of clarity may send you back to the starting point. If you start the search for your family history without clarity about who you are looking for, why you're looking for them, then you reduce your chances of getting off to a successful start. This can happen despite an initial burst of enthusiasm, commitment and energy.

How you begin depends on what you know about the things that are driving you. Give this some real thought before you line up for your race. It's part of your mental preparation.

The unanswerable questions need narrowing down until you are clear about the fundamental question you are trying to answer. Ask yourself the following: Is this a journey of self-discovery? Are you seeking information to help you better define who you are and from where you came. Are you interested in family characteristics? Perhaps there are certain physical and mental characteristics, which you share with other family members. It might be your nose, your mouth, your eyes, the texture of your hair, and even your complexion. You may wonder why certain members of the family have European features, whilst others have Asian and African features. Some family members may have a great sense of humour, while others are more reserved. Acknowledging characteristics that have been passed down the generations could bring into focus some of your key strengths – and possibly some characteristics you feel must be developed further.

Are you driven by the need to preserve legacy? Your family, on the whole, may have been achievers. They may have been first to do something unusual that has had an impact on the community in which they lived.

Which branch of the family tree interests you most? It could be your father line (your father's father's father...) or your mother line (your mother's mother's mother...).

Are you seeking to verify oral history? An older member of the family may have told you about the country, town or a time when key events in the family history took place. Despite this, you may have doubts about the accuracy of the story. Finding documentary evidence to validate the tale may be something that consumes your thoughts.

Where do your values come from? Your family may have approached life a little differently from other members of the community because of their core set of values and beliefs. Identifying where these values come from may help you to define better who you think you are.

These questions may trigger others. The important point is that success depends on clarity about the reasons for wishing to pursue your quest. Attempt to resolve only a few questions at a time. This will increase your chances of getting off to a good start. Narrow down the questions you wish answered to only one or two essential questions. The answers to these should determine how you proceed from here on in.

Breaking Down the Psychological Barriers to Moving Forward

A failure to plan is as good a plan as any plan to fail. The first stage of your quest, may well feel like rolling a heavy stone up a steep hill. By following a few simple rules, it could so easily feel like rolling a heavy stone down a gentle slope; hard work still, as there will be points along the way where the ground dips. However, the stone, as it gathers momentum in a downhill direction, will make the pushing feel a little easier. As with any type of human endeavour, mental preparation is an essential first step. Build your enthusiasm by thinking about all the obstacles you perceive are in your way. Then consider how best to overcome them.

Try not to get too bogged down in the things you think might prevent you from moving forwards. This could induce feelings of analysis paralysis.

Fear and anxiety about what you may or may not find can be a barrier to success. Always retain an open mind. The question you need to answer may be one that is shared by other family members – not just the elders but first cousins, second cousins, aunts and uncles. They may have heard stories but haven't necessarily found time to establish the truth of what was told.

Case Study I

I was born in Britain in 1964. My mother was born in 1941 at a place called Mount Pleasant in the parish of Portland, Jamaica. She immigrated to England in 1961 after being sent for by her father, who was already settled. I grew up knowing my maternal grandmother and my mother's siblings.

However, on my father's side, I knew very little. I never knew my paternal grandmother or grandfather. So I was naturally curious about my father's story. My father was born in Black River within the parish of St Elizabeth. He told me much about his upbringing in Jamaica. He was unable to tell me much about the family history, because his father died when he was only six years old. The reasons for undertaking this research were many and varied.

Self-discovery

I wanted to dig deep to understand profound feelings of rootlessness in my country of birth. My physical characteristics are clearly that of an African. But my name had European origins. Could I be the descendent of the European by the name of Crooks? Or was there some other reason why the family acquired this name.

Preserving legacy

I wanted to create a family tree and go back as far as I could go. My father is the first Jamaican in our lineage to arrive in England to settle. I liked to think that future generations would have an interest in his struggle to establish his family in England. My father always talked about the need to be independent. He told us never to borrow if we could help it and always pay back the very next day, if that were possible. He told us never to depend on anybody. He always stressed the importance of education. I want to know where these standards came from. To what extent did my grandfather imbue him with these values?

Finding a small part of a thousand-piece jigsaw puzzle is always going to be a reason to rejoice. Every new discovery provides a clue to the next. New discoveries can boost your desire to commit the time and energy necessary for achieving your aims in full.

Be careful when setting your goals. Try not to answer too many difficult questions. Going down this route will lead you to unrealistic expectations about what to look for. It is not realistic to set yourself the task of finding the slave ship that carried an ancestor to the Caribbean Islands 200 years ago. Few have been fortunate enough to have walked that path. The point is that it should not be the most pressing question at the start of your journey. As such, it should remain an aspiration, only to be targeted when the goal is in sight. You'll soon get a sense of what is realistic when you begin to understand what information exists and where it can be sourced.

Your next step should be to set some achievable goals. Here are a few simple rules about setting goals.

Specific: Be specific about what you want to achieve when taking that first vital step along the road to discovery. Setting yourself the task of finding your roots is courageous if not a little vague. Which roots are you looking for? Is it the great-grandmother that you heard childhood stories about? Is it the place where the family originated? Better to start by saying you wish to speak to all the elder members of the family before branching out. These are specific goals.

Measurable: This is about knowing what you will look for in order that you can confirm to yourself that you have achieved your goal. If your plan is to talk to members of the family then be clear in your mind how many. You may refine your goal, for example, by ensuring that you speak to the elder members of the family (specific) who are octogenarians (measurable) within six months.

Achievable: As your first step, you may decide that the first thing you will do is speak to a specific member of the family – perhaps an elder member. But how realistic is that as a first step if they live halfway across the world on a Caribbean island. Will you have the money at your disposal to go and meet them? You might refine your goal saying that you wish to speak to the elder members of the family (specific) who are octogenarians (measurable) within eighteen months (measurable and achievable).

Saving the money to visit relatives abroad is realistic only if you have the flow of income to enable you to pay for the trip. If you can make the trip, then ask yourself, is it realistic to expect more octogenarians to recall with lucidity the information to the level of detail that will satisfy you. Some memories may have started to fade with age. Try refining your goal to speaking to elder members of the family (specific), who are octogenarians (measurable) within 18 months (measurable, achievable and realistic), provided they are willing and able to talk about the past (realistic).

Time: whatever you decide to do, always place time limits on it. Think about when you want to start your research. As soon as possible might be well-intentioned, but it may not be measurable. Starting tomorrow may well be well-intentioned, measurable and specific, but how realistic is it.

You've identified an aim. For example: to find the year a maternal grandparent arrived in England. Then try finding out as much about your maternal grandparent, before she settled in England. Use the following approach:

New Year's resolution	To find out when grandmother was born
By when	Within the next two weeks
How would I know when I've done enough	A phone call to mother

That First Go at Creating a Family Tree

Family trees are great for summarising information and presenting it in an appealing format. You should have a go at putting pen to paper sketching the tree at the earliest opportunity. The process of doing this would help boost your motivation and desire to follow through to the end.

Start by putting down on paper some key personal facts. Begin with full name, date of birth and place of birth, important milestones in your life. Do the same for your parents and work backwards in time. The further back you go, the more you will understand what you know, what you do not know and what interests you most. Names, dates and places are the minimum basic requirements when pulling information into a family tree.

Produce a rough sketch of your family tree as soon as you can. Take time to think about the people you know least about. Try to imagine the events that shaped their lives; the decisions they made, the actions they took, the challenges they faced that may explain the environment you find yourself in today. Would your forebears have led reasonably stable lives? Are theirs the stories of rags to riches?

You should aim to find out as much as you can about one or two individuals within your tree that you know least about. Aim to fill the information gaps. Starting your family tree at the earliest possible opportunity helps you to clarify your aims and to set achievable goals.

It's often the case that information is written down and simply lost. It can be incredibly frustrating should you decide, after you have achieved much, that you wish to remind yourself where it all started! So, when you finish your first sketch, put it in an envelope or folder and file it carefully. Look at it every now and then to remind yourself why you produced it and what you were setting out to achieve.

In time you will have gathered information to answer many of those answerable questions. You will look back at your sketch and remember with a high level of satisfaction when it all began in earnest.

Case Study 2

Aim: To find my African ancestor, the first person in our family along the male line to bear the name Crooks.

How did I get started? I set myself realistic objectives at every stage. There were eight objectives in total over the thirteen years it took me to trace my origins. As each objective was achieved, the impossible began to feel possible. I set my objectives in the following order:

Objective 1: to find my grandfather's birth certificate. I knew this would confirm my great-grandfather's name – my father was a young child when he died. The first step was to talk to the elders. I obtained his date of birth from them, in addition to his full name. With that information, I visited the family history centre in London to trace his birth certificate. When I found it, the birth certificate revealed the name of my great-grandfather, Robert Crooks.

Objective 2: to find the baptism records for Robert Crooks.

Objective 3: to find records of my great-great-grandfather.

Objective 4: to find records of my great-great-great-grandfather.

Objective 5: to discover the location of the sugar plantation where they laboured.

Objective 6: to discover what the slave registers could tell me about my great-great-great-grandfather.

Objective 7: to understand why my great great-great-grandmother was included in the baptism records as a resident of Cousins Cove, but was included in the slave register as the mother of slave children and not as a slave.

Objective 8: to find my great-great-great-great-grandmother's origins in Africa.

Oral Tradition: the Key to Unlocking the Past

Why Is It So important?

Oral tradition is a word-of-mouth media. History, folktales and values are passed down from generation to generation in this way. Young people as the heirs to the family legacy are potential custodians of hundreds of years of family history. A conscious effort is needed by family members to reinvent oral history and supplement the technology now available to help keep the legacy alive.

Africans are revered storytellers. Traditions are passed on using a variety of verbal communication tools: tales, folktales, myth and so on. One of the most important people in African society was the griot – a historian and storyteller.

The history of Africa as given to us has been reliant to a greater extent on written evidence. But Africans had their own particular system of recording past events, situations and traditions, before Europeans started writing about it. This was based on collecting oral testimonies.

Most Western societies regarded this method untrustworthy as a means of gathering and preserving information. As a result, non-African historians used written documentation to chart the history of the continent. If this was missing, it was assumed that nothing worth recording had happened.[7]

Griots were trained to recount the genealogy, or family history, of everyone in the village going back centuries. Before the histories are written they must be told. A griot, in preparation for death, passes on the entire historical account to a younger man or woman. In turn, they would become the new historian in the family for the village. A griot retained all the facts and important events of their time: tales, myths, fables and songs are all part of the oral tradition. Tales handed down the generations are told with a strong flavour of moral and political instruction.

Information-gathering begins with what you know about you, your parents and grandparents. Names of family members, dates of birth, and places of residence are essential if you are planning to undertake research at public records.

Think about things you know about yourself, such as characteristics shared with other family members. Clarity should follow reflection on the sort of conversations that you may wish to have with family members. You should aim to talk to relatives, family friends, associates or neighbours who can provide insights about forebears with whom you hold similar characteristics: 'You laugh like your granddad's brother'; 'You are as stubborn as your grandfather.'

Spontaneous comments during the course of a conversation can open the door to wide-ranging discussions about family. It can provide clues about where to go for the next piece in the jigsaw. A distant family member may already have identified useful information. They may welcome the opportunity to pass the baton to you to take the next leg of the journey.

If you are seeking identity and a better understanding of who you are, then you may find great value in seeking more impartial, warts and all commentary. Family friends or extended members of the family are probably best. They can be incredibly frank and informative when giving opinions of your relatives. They may be willing and able to talk about issues or a side of someone's character that other family members have elected to not speak about. It's extremely important because it may help explain some of the things you've always known about yourself and how you may be perceived by others. Think about it, at one time or another, your forebear may have been perceived as aggressive, rude, arrogant by some and as gentle, hard-working or kind by others. This is possible, if they were able to change according to who they were dealing with. You might interpret these characteristics as evidence of the family's spirit of resistance and independence. You may relate to some or all and wish to modify certain aspects of your behaviour according to what you learn about your forebear. You may even decide you want to accentuate them. Perhaps you have been unaware of disease in your family such as diabetes; and that your relative suffered the loss of sight or limbs having failed to recognise the symptoms early enough to take action to prevent it happening in the first place. In these circumstances, be prepared to act to reduce the risks of acquiring the disease and reducing your quality of life.

But I Have No Information About Father or Mother?

If you were raised in a single-parent household, you may have very little information about one of your parents. It would be important to find out their full name. If you can, try to get an idea of approximately when they were born. If you cannot get either, then try to find out as much as you can about any marriage history. Documents concerning these events will reveal a wealth of information that could lead you to other sources about them (see the section on marriage records).

Find out where they were born or where they grew up. Relatives, friends of the family or previous work associates should be found and interviewed. Relatives and friends may have an idea of when they came. They may have spoken about the ship that they arrived on. Some may have travelled on the same ship, or know others that did. If your mother or father moved around the UK there is likely to be a record of them in public records. If you're able to engage them in conversation, it is important that you identify the parish, district or town where they were born or brought up. If they embarked from the Caribbean to come to the UK, then you should try to obtain the following information:

* Full name;
* The port within the Caribbean from which they embarked;
* The port within the UK at which they disembarked;
* The year or decade they arrived;
* Skills/profession/other work that they may have been previously engaged in;
* Where they lived when they first came to the UK including address;
* The ship that carried them.

All or some of the above will assist in a fruitful search of passenger list records and may even increase the chances of finding a birth record (see the section on immigration records and passenger lists).

Making the Best Use of Relatives
By interviewing as many family members as possible you set a solid foundation for achieving success in your search. You should be seeking to obtain as much information as you can from them. Be aware, it can be equally rewarding if you make a point of sharing, with your family members, anything that you have discovered along the way. Not only does this help your relatives to gain more knowledge of the past, it also helps them to feel involved in the process of preserving the family legacy.

Talk to relatives in their home, but there are a few things to think about before arranging visits. First, elders are more likely to talk openly about their memories if they have a high level of trust in you as a person. Establishing relationships, mutual trust and interest will pay dividends in the long run. Say why it's important that you meet, explaining the advantages to the family of record- ing and preserving information about their lives. They may see the benefit and associate a level of prestige in the use of their life stories in instructing the younger generation. Make it clear that it is your wish, amongst others, to protect the integrity of the infor- mation that you receive. Generate enthusiasm by telling them what you are doing, where you've got to and that you need their help to further your research. Also consider using the process in facilitating a reunion with a relative your interviewee may have been longing to see.

Maart is an old African tradition, where young people, out of respect for the elders, have to ask permission to speak. This ancient African tradition facilitated the transfer of knowledge, skills and experience from older generations to the young. In parts of the so-called 'developed world', it is commonplace for children to interrupt adult conversation. In doing so, they miss opportuni- ties to learn things they cannot learn in other environments.

Most elders have more time to spend with young people than they did with their own children. Time spent sitting with an elder, listening to them use words to paint stories of the past, is research time well spent, particularly when elders enjoy interacting with close members of the family. Approaching an elder you may not have spoken to for many years may present certain challenges. More so, if you are hoping that they will share family memorabilia with you. Face-to-face contact is a positive factor in unlocking information about the past.

Ephemera can be powerful for invoking conversations. Equip yourself with information you have already gathered: old family photographs, diaries, passports, your sketch of the family tree, and other types of documentation are great for reminiscence. Revealing information that you already have in your possession conveys your noble intentions. A passport picture can trigger a story about embarkation from the Caribbean Islands at the time it was taken. A cursory look at the clothes worn by a relative in the picture can trigger thoughts about the life and times.

Begin by talking about some of the things you already know about the photograph. You should do so in a way that enables the relative to validate what you are saying. Listen for responses such as 'that's right' or 'that's true'.

Elders will often jump from one era to another; if you have the collection of items then arrange them chronologically. This will help you identify where, along timeline, the conversation has reached. If you have developed your skills as an interviewer, you can reset the conversation to a different point along the timeline.

Listen carefully to how elders refer to particular relatives. For example, nieces and nephews may refer to Grandfather by one name, while friends may use another when speaking of him. Prompted by information about which they had a previous recollection, they may be able to throw in some knowledge that completes the picture. It is possible that they may contradict some of the things you've told them by recalling another version of events. There is usually no smoke without fire so verify as much as you can. It is possible to obtain some clarity by contradicting their version of events. Try describing ancestor's characteristics inaccurately. Watch for your interviewee's reaction. They might leap at the opportunity to correct you if they think someone has misinformed you. In correcting you, they may provide you with an abundance of evidence to support their recollection of events.

Approach interviews with tact and diplomacy. Elders may have experiences locked away which they may be unwilling to talk about. Always respect their wishes. Also the flow of conversation may be inhibited by the presence of certain individuals from whom they may prefer to withhold information. Consider carefully the approach you take when dealing with such situations.

The process itself could trigger moments of quiet reflection – perhaps a review of their life. Remember, your inquiries could be about issues where few have shown interest. So be sensible about how you handle interviews.

The interview should be a pleasurable experience for the interviewees. Encourage them to talk generally about the past when initiating conversation. For example, school days, leaving home, growing up with their siblings, the day they left for England, the day they arrived and the difficulty of settling in a foreign land.

The interview shouldn't feel like an interrogation, so make sure you avoid concentrating heavily on events that your subject is plainly not interested in discussing. Ask permission to talk about anything you feel might be sensitive. Also, be sure the person understands the reason you are asking. Let them know why it is important for you to know. If they express an unspoken wish to be silent on an issue then refrain from pursuing your line of questioning. Some memories may be too painful, or embarrassing, to resurrect – particularly if it shows the family in a bad light. Be discreet about how you use the information you've obtained and avoid stirring up old resentments.

Tape-recorded conversations are an obvious way of capturing information. A word of warning, however: this can be challenging if you have not invested in expensive tape-recording equipment. Apart from trouble picking up sound and playing it back, your interviewee may not feel comfortable talking into the recording machine. This may stunt the flow of information, and your interviewee may even clam up.

Camcorders can be good at picking up sound from reasonable distances, although the quality of the sound can deteriorate outside an enclosed area. Far from clamming up, your interviewee may be inclined to perform for the camera. They may spice up stories because they know they might enjoy seeing the whole thing played back to them later on.

Develop your interview technique to a level at which you're

able to maintain your interviewee's interest in the subject matter. Annotate any new information they provide to you on an early sketch that you've made of a family tree. Resist the urge to take notes of everything your interviewee says. This can lead to lots of repetition. If you must have things repeated then do so by asking the same question differently. The key is to understand the gist of what they're saying. When you understand this, then you're better placed to recall the facts later when reviewing your notes. If at all possible take another interested member of the family with you to help you take notes.

Whatever you do, make sure your interviewee is comfortable with you recording information in this way. Another word of warning: minor details that you do not think important can turn out to be real gems later on.

Aim to finish the conversations within a reasonable time. Gently wind down the conversation when you are satisfied that you have all that you need. Reliving the past can be difficult for some. For elders, the interview can feel exhausting. So it is important not to leave them lost in the past. Spend a little bit of time drawing them back to the present by talking about other present-day issues relevant to them.

It is possible that all your questions may not have been answered during the first visit. Save something for another time. By doing so, you give yourself the chance to reflect on the interview and think of new avenues of inquiry.

The following is intended to help structure the interview. These are also leading questions, or questions intended to open up a discussion. Relatives may not be sure about exact dates. You should not be overly concerned with this, for there are ways of getting around it. It may be possible to work out dates from research at the National Archives and libraries depending on what they say about the life and times in which your forebears lived. For example, you may hope to find a record of your father's immigration to England. Your mother may not know when your father

Case Study 3

Aim: To find out as much as I could about my grandfather by visiting elders in Jamaica who might have known him.

I spent two years planning my visit to Jamaica in 1990. The purpose of the visit was twofold. The family hadn't visited for almost ten years. So this was intended as a family holiday, and all that that entailed. The family reunion was held at the house of one of my aunts after the church service. When everybody was gathered I took the opportunity to ask my aunt about the family history. Like my father, she did not know much, but was able to signpost me to three elders who had attended.

The first lady she pointed out to me was an aunt aged seventy-seven at the time. She was one that my father had never mentioned, and therefore one I had never met. I discovered that she was my father's half-sister. He had had little knowledge of her. I introduced myself and immediately began probing. It was soon clear that her memories were fading. There were some photographs on hand and with gentle encouragement, I was able to extract some valuable information. I discovered that she was not the only half sibling, but that she had an older brother named John – my grandfather's first son. What I hadn't appreciated at the time, but would discover later in the research process, was that John was the most significant of the names in the paternal line going back many generations. She also provided the name of my grandmother and her sisters. And for the first time I learned of our connections with Cuba, the place where my grandparents first met.

The second was my father's eldest sister. She was very quietly spoken, dignified, if not a little reserved – not one to embellish stories. She had knowledge of my grandfather's birthday. She also knew my great-grandfather's name and also the name of my great-great-grandmother. She was also the source of information about his character. Her husband was more outgoing, insomuch that he loved talking about the Crooks family and laughing at memories of his interaction with the elders when he was a young man. My father and I sat with him for a long time, until the sun went down. Listening to him talking about my grandfather and the times in his life was a treat. He talked and we listened, punctuating with the odd question here and there. He was able to give context and therefore life to the grandfather I had never met. When I left I felt that a huge gap had been filled. My father was present, and he was able to exercise great judgement and skill in listening and being able to time questions appropriately so as not to significantly interrupt the flow.

Uncle (as we called him) talked fondly about my grandfather's youngest brother. It struck me that everybody is different, and this side of the family enjoyed talking about the past and gossiping light-heartedly. The gossip was always interesting and unwittingly they were helping me to understand much about myself and the way we are as a family.

Subsequently, when I came back to England, we made contact with my father's first cousin, an elder with a passion for the family and humour to match. He was able to add to all that I had learned.

immigrated but she may be certain it was a few months after the war, or weeks before the Queen's coronation. This information in itself will provide you with approximate dates from which you can develop your research inquiry.

Political Factors
Find out as much as you can about the political landscape before he/she arrived:

* What was the political party in power at the time?
* Did we have any relatives who participated in politics/unions?
* Which political party did the family support?
* Which member of the family was most vocal about politics?
* Which members of the family avoided politics?

Economic Factors
* What was life like?

* Did the family want for anything: a car, a fridge, electricity or food?
* How was it overcome?
* What do you remember about the houses you lived in?
* How did you get money to pay for books?
* Who worked and where?
* How did parents behave (punish/reward) towards their young in those days?

Social and Cultural Factors
* What was the dominant religion?
* Were there any other religions?
* What were the attitudes towards these other religions?
* What were the attitudes towards other people who came from other countries?
* Did you learn to speak other languages at school?
* What games did people play?
* What did men do that they don't do today?

Technological Factors
* Did they have electricity in those days?
* How were shoes and clothes made?
* How did people get from one place to another?

The elders within the family are primary sources of information. They would have known your recent forebears. Their eyes would have seen the light of events that happened decades before your birth. They would have heard conversations that will never be heard again. Their minds are books which must be opened to understand all that took place before videos and audio equipment were so easy to purchase.

The elders must be treated as delicately as a rare book. History resides in their heads. When an elder passes on, their knowledge goes with them and can never be retrieved.

Public Records and Their Hidden Treasures

The interviews you may have conducted with family and friends should give you the best possible start in creating a family tree. Your tree – which may still be a rough sketch – would contain names, dates of birth (approximate in some cases) and places of birth. You will begin to see clearly the gaps in your information. Names, dates and place of birth are your passports to the past. When you have these, you are ready to research the public records.

* The full name including middle names can be instrumental in helping you to distinguish between two individuals with the same Christian and surnames.
* Birth dates help you to distinguish between individuals who were born in the same location with the same name.
* Place of birth helps distinguish between individuals with the same name and year of birth/baptism.

Many records you will find are organised by parish or administered areas. You should aim to determine what sources to interrogate. How useful are they likely to be? You simply won't know until you've explored. It really depends on the challenges you have set yourself and how specific, measurable, achievable, realistic and time related they are (see previous chapter).

This section focuses on the sources of information and how to make the best use of them.

You should prepare to visit public records as soon as you feel you have obtained all that you can from family and friends. If you have reached this stage already, then rejoice in the achievement. Not only will you have good information to pursue your quest in earnest, you will also have the level of motivation and commitment necessary to embark on this challenging phase of the discovery process.

The Internet

Most islands in the Caribbean will keep records of their past – some will be better and therefore easier to access than others. If you're committed to going down this road, be sure you have prepared adequately beforehand. Use the Internet to find out what is available online or locally. If it is the case that you have to travel to a particular archive in question, then at least you'll know sooner rather than later of its potential to provide documentation to assist you in your search.

The Internet hosts thousands of sites on family history. New sites come and go so frequently, making it a pointless exercise listing them in this book. There are some sites that are more popular than others. You would probably be better off accessing a couple of the sites that have been around for some time, to gain access to the plethora of links that are out there in cyberspace. It also helps to structure your search so that you gain access to those sites that could potentially answer your questions. **Afrigenas. com**, **Rootsweb.com**, **Ancestry.co.uk** and **Genealogy.com** host lots of links to other sites. You'll get to your destination quickly enough by typing any of these names into your search engine.

Afrigenas.com and Genealgy.com have a particularly good worldwide genealogy forum. The forum can help you engage with a community of family historians seeking those vital pieces of information about their Caribbean Island histories. You can post your questions on the site of your choice using email. You can, if you wish, also help others with problems they will have encountered.

Ancestry.co.uk have been reproducing slave registers online. Be aware that many sites offering such information charge a fee for doing so.

The Internet can also help with the following:

* Preparing for visits to national and local repositories and archives;
* Finding specific information about an ancestor;
* Finding information about what public records are held and where;
* Finding forums or message boards offering information and advice that are useful for specific questions and answers;
* General information on local history, community and family;
* Finding what information is actually out there in the public domain.

You could use the Internet to get information on European migrations to the Caribbean. For example, you might be interested in finding out about a German ancestor who may have migrated to the Caribbean Islands. A quick search could help you determine how much Germanic migration actually took place and where they settled. You may find it useful to establish the embarkation points, and explore the possibilities for finding documentation at those ports. One line of inquiry may indeed lead to another.

The Internet is simple to use. If you've never used the Internet or a computer before, then think about inquiring with your local authority regarding enrolment on an adult education course. You could have fun meeting people on these courses, if nothing else!

Case Study 4

My grandfather's full name was Christopher Maitland Crooks. I was always curious about why the middle name, Maitland, was chosen, as it was an uncommon name. By searching the Internet using the keywords "Maitland Jamiaca" I discovered that someone had already undertaken extensive research on the Maitlands of Westmoreland. I discovered that the Maitlands were affluent landowners. From this information I gained some clues as to how my grandfather and his siblings may have come by large plots of land during the nineteenth century.

The Family History Centres

The Church of Jesus Christ of Latter-day Saints, also known as the Mormons, have centres in major cities around the world. Their head office is based in Salt Lake City, Utah. The church collects and maintains the largest collection of family history information in the world. You do not have to be a member of the church to use their facilities, and the service is free to the public.

The Mormons believe 'that family love and life can continue forever, even after death. Through ordinances they bind together families, husband and wife, and children to parents, in order to spend eternity together. They also believe that these ordinances should be performed on behalf of ancestors who did not have the opportunity to do so themselves. Ancestors are not forced to take the ordinances; they must accept the opportunity to do so'. But before members can help their ancestors, they must identify them, and that is why they are engaged in recording family histories across the world.

Baptism, marriage and death records, Caribbean

The British government needed to be kept informed of activities within the islands under British control. The government therefore required meticulous reporting arrangements by the assemblies in its colonies. The format was usually similar to that of comparable records collected within mainland Britain.

In 1597 during the reign of Henry VII, an Act of Parliament was passed in England and Wales when Thomas Cromwell decreed that the clergy should record baptisms, marriages and burials in every parish. Basic information was written down in the book after service on Sunday in the presence of churchwardens. In 1597, Queen Elizabeth I decreed that all existing records should be copied into 'fair parchment books'. Ecclesiastical parish registers are the most important of all records if you are embarking on a search.

Parish registers were handwritten ledgers. They recorded births, baptisms, marriages, deaths and burials in named administered areas (the equivalent of districts, boroughs or county councils). The information contained within the registers themselves may vary from parish to parish and country to country. It means that some registers contain a wealth of information while others may leave you wanting for more.

The parish records for the Caribbean Islands from 1800 onwards are of interest because they contain records of mass slave baptisms. These are usually listings of the names of slaves baptised on a particular date on a given plantation. Individual records can number in excess of 100 for medium to large plantations. Some mass baptisms were not included for certain parish records.

From 1813, parish baptismal records include father's occupation and abode. By 1813 marriage records included father's name and occupation.

Parish registers are the most relevant source of information up until 1880 for the British Caribbean Islands, after which the records change to civil records (see section on civil registers). The islands of the British West Indies registered births, marriages and deaths in relatively consistent format, as required by the British government. Births were registered according to the district where they took place. This may not necessarily have been within the village or hamlet where the child actually lived but possibly within walking distance of it.

Registration records presumably do not exist where people had to endure long distances through inaccessible routes. Also, literacy rates during the decades that followed emancipation may explain the low uptake on birth and baptism registration. Few people would have been willing to lay bare the lack of instruction in reading and writing. Some may not have travelled to the district registry offices because they did not see it as a major priority.

There are more names in baptismal records than appear in the records of marriages and deaths. This may be because registration was part of the celebration and recognition of a birth in African communities. Others may simply have anticipated the importance of retaining paper records, conscious of the value property owners would have placed on the official documents, especially in the years following emancipation.

Baptismal records are perhaps the most important documents to look at if you are to discover the identities of ancestors once held in bondage. Plantation owners in the British colonies promoted the belief that Africans and their descendents were subhuman. The prevailing logic of the slave-owning classes, at the time, was that Africans and their descendents could not take on religion as a result of this perceived inferiority. Not content in their belief, they implemented legal barriers to prevent Quakers, Methodists, Baptists and German-Moravians from proselytising to slaves. They feared Africans acquiring religion because it followed that they would be able to build a common language and a common set of beliefs. Were this to happen then they would naturally organise themselves around these common beliefs and a common cause – the pursuit of freedom by any means necessary. For this reason there were few baptism records relating to Africans in the first half of the 1700s. The records that do exist relate to European settlers including children the masters fathered with Africans in bondage.

Non-conformist Baptist preachers entered the island in the latter parts of the eighteenth century and during the nineteenth century. By this time, the descendents of Africans (the so-called Creole black/negro classes) had acquired English as their first language. They were required to learn English as a part of the process referred to as seasoning (forced acceptance of their environment). Earlier fears of what would follow were realised with an upsurge in organised freedom movements on a small scale. This represented a threat to the British way of life in the Caribbean. The church was seen as the best chance the slave-owning classes had of pacifying slaves. Towards the latter half of the eighteenth century increasing numbers of Africans and their descendants were baptised. Early on, in the 1800s, mass baptisms increased. As many as 300 slaves could be baptised in a single ceremony. Records of some, but not all, baptisms exist at the family history centres. There are other institutions that contain records of baptisms such as the National Archives.

Notes about baptism records
The baptism records are an important source of information about births. By considering the information they contain alongside other information which you may have gathered (oral accounts, records about other members of the family) you can approximate the year of birth. Some baptism records may indicate the age at baptism. But the first thing to understand is that they cannot be relied upon to give the actual date of birth – unlike birth certificates. This is because baptisms generally took place weeks, months and sometimes years after the birth of a child.

Baptism records are important for another reason. As with birth certificates of today, they usually contained the names of the child's parents. As such they provide a stepping stone to the previous generation. This makes them the most important avenue of exploration after you have exhausted interviews with family and friends of the family.

The following is a return as copied from the parish register and the estate's books of slaves baptised in the parish of Hanover, Jamaica, by the Reverend Daniel Warner Rose, rector in the years 1814–1816 and up to 20 June 1817.[8] It includes the names of the properties and the proprietors to whom they belonged, and the time they were baptised.

Properties or place of baptism	Proprietors	Number baptised	When baptised
At Cousins Cove	R. Dickson Esq.	184	April 3, 1814
At Cousins Cove	W. Brown	22	April 3, 1814

If you are lucky enough to locate an ancestor's record dated prior to 1838 and containing a place of baptism, then celebrate the fact that you would also have successfully identified the plantation on which they lived and worked. A discovery of this kind could open up a treasure of information about your history.

Law 6 registers

Parish records take you up to 1870–72, but overlap with what are called Law 6 registers. These government registers began in 1866, and they ceased when civil registration was introduced. Law 6 registers are separated into births, marriages and deaths and have also been microfilmed. There are separate indexes for Law 6 registers in catalogues available at the Church of the Latter-day Saints family history centres. The indexes will signpost you to original records where they exist.[9]

Civil registers

Civil registration of births, marriages and deaths started in England and Wales on 1 July 1837. Up until then, only the registers of the established church were accepted as a legal record. As the number of non-conformist churches began to grow in Britain as well as the Caribbean, the parish registers became more and more incomplete.

In the early nineteenth century a House of Commons committee recommended that the local system be replaced by a national system of registration and that a civil marriage ceremony be introduced. On 1 July 1837, in the first year of Queen Victoria's reign, the new modern registration service began. This was later expanded in 1927 to also include stillbirths and adoptions.

Civil registration began in Scotland in 1855, in Ireland in 1863 and the Caribbean in 1880 where they are catalogued by parish. Within a parish there were many districts identified in the indexes constructed by the family history centres, so make sure you have located the right district when placing your order. The indexes are a little confusing at first. When you look at them often enough and scroll through the microfilms to which they point, you begin to understand their relevance and importance in helping you to locate information. The key is to persevere with them.

Family history centres hold civil registration records for some Caribbean islands on microfilm. Be warned, some of these records are incomplete in terms of the years held. If the family history centres do not hold what you're looking for then you may have to journey to the island's national archive to complete your search. Dealing with staff in some areas of administration can be a challenge. Patience, tact, diplomacy and persistence may be the key attributes to carry you forward.

The family history centres have created indexes for the civil registers which contain the names of individuals issued with birth certificates. Actual birth certificates are held in microfilm, each of which can hold up to three years' worth of birth certificates.

The Church of the Latter-day Saints has microfilmed some of the records held at archives on Caribbean islands. There are indexes to the civil registers, which are arranged by parish, and by first letter of surname. The registers are filed under the names of each parish or locality.

Birth certificates are important because they contain the following information:

Your parents':

* Names;
* Dates of birth;
* Places of birth;
* Their father's name and surname;
* Their mother's name and maiden name;
* Their father's occupation;
* The date of registration;
* The place where they were registered.

Marriage certificates provide a similar set of information.

* The dates they were married;
* Your parents' names and surnames;
* Their ages;
* Descriptions;
* Professions;
* Place of residence;
* Names of your grandparents;
* Occupation of grandparents;
* Name of witness.

Death certificates: If you're able to trace a death certificate, then you will find the following information.

* Name;

* Surname;
* Age at death;
* Occupation;
* Cause of death;
* Name of informer;
* Dates of registration;
* Date of death.

Finding your way around the records at family history centres

The indexes are organised geographically according to parish and then district location (see section on the Royal Geographical Society). It is important that you have a good idea where your ancestor was born before you visit a centre. Prepare for visits by going online to the family history centres. You can perform limited searches online. It is possible to order films from the church's head office in Salt Lake City, Utah, USA, if you find that the record you are looking for is not held in your local family history centre.

Royal Geographical Society

Details of full names, dates of baptism and marriage, death records and geographical location will help you to confirm the existence of your ancestor. However, you may feel a natural yearning to uncover something about their life and times.

It is at this point that maps and surveys are powerful tools helping you to reconstruct the political, economic, social, technological and cultural environment. You may begin to wonder about the paths they trod, the hills they climbed, the soils they farmed and the places where they worked. You can begin to get a visual sense of their reality by looking at maps of how things may have been. You may decide to pursue new avenues of inquiry about places long forgotten.

Maps can throw light on the geographical location of a settlement where your ancestor may once have lived. This increases

Case Study 5

I began inquiring about my grandfather as a young child. I learned that he died when my father was very young. For much of my young adult life, I never thought it would be possible to trace any documentation relating to him.

On discovering the parish records, I managed to trace my father line (my father's father's father and so on) to the early 1800s. To trace my father line was a good move, because the name Crooks is uncommon. This meant that I had more of a chance of finding Crookses that were likely to be related in Westmoreland. I had also appreciated that the surname is passed down through the male line.

The Church of the Latter-day Saints (LDS) in London kept microfilm records of Jamaican births, marriages and deaths originating from the Spanish Town Archives, Jamaica. The records are organised according to Jamaican parish and then chronologically. The films for records post-1877 are held at the centre in Salt Lake City, Utah. I ordered a film containing birth records for Westmoreland, 1886. To do this, I completed a simple form and paid a small fee for the cost of postage and packaging. Approximately four week later, LDS London sent a notice telling me that the film had arrived. I found a film copy of my grandfather's birth certificate. His birth was registered at a place called Bigwoods, just outside Darliston town; furthermore, it confirmed Robert as my great-grandfather and Caroline Dell as my great-grandmother.

I started by familiarising myself with indexes, but these do not provide detailed information. They are listings, like the contents of a book. They are merely signposts to the more detailed information. The indexes enabled me to quickly compile a list of people with the name Crooks, who were possibly my ancestors.

Record of baptism			Folio	Page
Clarke	1868	Janet	17	305
Crooks		Robert	17	305

Record of baptism			Folio	Page
Campbell		James M.	17	314
Cummings		Charles J.	17	315
Coates		William B.	17	316
Crowe	1865	Archibald	18	317
Clayton		Princess Louise	18	317
Coates		Charlotte	18	318

I recorded the film references and/or the folio numbers. I was then able to search through the ledger and find the names that were of interest to me. It is important to keep a record of the reference numbers, in case you do not have the time to look at all the records in the same visit. In my case return visits were indeed necessary.

The death records were of limited use for my particular search. I was unable to discover anything concrete about the deaths of any of my ancestors from the death records. The centre, I realised, did not hold copies of documents for the decades that interested me. That would require a visit to the archives in Jamaica.

The records I found were as follows:

Relationship	Name	Document	Year	Reference
Grandfather	Christopher Crooks	Birth certificate	1886	*FHL INTL Film 1523337 Items: 14–19*
Great-grandfather	Robert Crooks	Baptism record	1868	Microfilm index: 1291720 Volume: 17 folio: 305
Great-great-grandfather	William Crooks	Baptism record and marriage certificate	1834 1855	Microfilm Index: 122432 Volume: 2 Folio: 288

>

Relationship	Name	Document	Year	Reference
Great-great-great-grandfather, Great-great-great-grandmother and children	John Alexander Crooks and Sarah Brown	Baptism record	1814 1834	Microfilm Index: 122432 Volume: 2 Folio: 288

I also found:

* The marriage listing of my great-great-grandfather William Crooks to Ellen.
* A record of only three Crooks between 1806 and 1838 in Westmoreland (though none were related).
* Baptism records for dozens more Crooks prior to 1838 in Hanover, going as far back as 1700.
* William's baptism in 1834 along with his two siblings: John, aged eight and Barbary, aged four.
* Those baptised had been classified according to 'degrees' of racial mix, such as negro, mulatto, quadroon, mustee, white.
* A film recording many of the mass baptisms of slaves in the parish of Hanover. Most took place on large properties prior to 1821. Frustratingly there was no record of the mass baptism that I later found had taken place on Cousins Cove.
* Great-great-great-grandparents John Crooks and Sarah Brown lived on the Cousins Cove plantation.
* John was an unskilled labourer.
* John Alexander Crooks's baptism on 1 January 1813.

I used the centre to obtain a listing for the specific information contained within each of the parish records, post-1877. I was able to photocopy this list for a small sum of money. On reading the list it became clear to me that a microfilm existed for Darliston, Westmoreland, Jamaica, 1886 (the dates of my grandfather's birth). Nowadays, information about the contents held on microfilm can be obtained from the Internet, so you can prepare your own prints.

the possibilities for attributing value and meaning to the social problems that existed in those times. Understanding the movements of your ancestors from one place to another, provides an appreciation of how movement and communication between communities spread further afield, had been restricted. It also increases the understanding of how it was that the Caribbean Islands were systematically underdeveloped despite the major contributions they made to the American mainland and Europe.

Changes of name, ownership and function of plantations and towns can be insightful. Maps can inform on people who settled the Caribbean. They can help provide evidence to confirm whether your family name is originated from that of a proprietor who lived during the seventeenth, eighteenth and nineteenth centuries. You may also use maps to trace the location of properties they once owned. Supplemented by research at local archives and libraries, you could find yourself rediscovering local history of communities that lived in settlements that sprung up all over the Caribbean following emancipation.

If you can trace back to a specific geographical location in the Caribbean, then it is worth making a point of visiting the location. It might be a property way up in the hills, a plantation near the coast or a cattle pen further inland. The chances are that much will have changed over the decades since many of the sugar, coffee and pimento plantations were wound down. Preparation is essential if you're going to make sense of the visit. If at all possible, take with you copies of maps, topography, estate surveys, newspaper articles and so on. B.W. Higman describes how the above plantations would have been laid out and the type of activities that your ancestors may have been engaged in.

A visit to a plot of land could be useful in helping you to visualise the location of the proprietor's house on the hill, the location of Africans/Asians and their descendants within slave villages

Case Study 6

I had spent some time researching my father line when I hit a barrier that proved difficult to overcome. There were records of a number of individuals in the parish of Westmoreland bearing the surname Crooks from 1838 onwards. There were only three prior to that date, and none of them were related.

It was a chance conversation with a colleague at work, who told me that she had a grandmother bearing the same surname. She told me that her grandmother came from a neighbouring parish to Westmoreland. The penny dropped when I realised that 1838 was the date that Africans held in bondage were free to leave the plantations and set up communities elsewhere.

Looking at the different maps of Jamaica helped me appreciate how migrations across the island from parish to parish would have been constrained by the geography. Most of the plantation activity was around the coastal areas. You do not have to travel far inland before you hit steep mountain precipices and hills. I speculated that former slaves would journey, perhaps as far as a neighbouring parish and no further, if they were going to set up life anew. Few would have had sufficient transport to take themselves and a few belongings beyond the confines of the plantation. It seemed all the more logical when the geography of Jamaica is examined. Most people would have travelled by horse and cart (wagons) up until and beyond the 1950s. Ex-slaves took to the hills to capture plots of land in uncharted hills and mountains.

The story of my ancestor's migration had made much more sense. The next generation of Crooks moved no more than twenty miles further south towards Darliston and the plains of Westmoreland. Within two generations, they had moved another twenty miles to settle in the town of Black River on the south coast of Jamaica.

and burial grounds, as well as the siting of mills and cane fields. If you prepare carefully, then there is every chance you will identify evidence of the settlement that once existed.

The main public records offices organise records by parish. Thereafter, records are organised chronologically and then alphabetically. Be mindful that parishes may have changed or moved boundaries over the years since their inception. Some have been created whilst others have ceased to exist. Parishes are only administrative areas, and administrative areas change according to the needs perceived by the bureaucrats of the time. An awareness of parish changes will increase your chances of success. In 1814 there were twenty-one parishes in Jamaica, which included those with names such as St David, St Dorothy, St George, St Thomas in the East, St Thomas in the Vale, Vere & St John. All of these have been absorbed within the present-day parishes of which there are now only fourteen. Why is this so important? Well, through your oral research, someone may have told you that they came from the parish of Clarendon in Jamaica. They're unlikely to have appreciated that Clarendon was once divided into four parishes: St John, St Dorothy, Vere and Clarendon. The town they say they came from may well be filed under a parish that did not exist a generation or two after their birth. This is why it is important for you to familiarise yourself with maps indicating the old administrative areas.

The Royal Geographical Society (RGS), Kensington Gore, London, holds maps and documents forming one of the most important geographical collections in the world. They have collected over two million maps, but you needn't be put off by this. Some maps date back many decades. The RGS also holds original antique printed maps of the West Indies. A limited range of materials can be requested by prior appointment only.

All of the material held by the RGS can be viewed online.[10] There are maps of Caribbean islands identifying the names of the slave-owning proprietors. You can find maps indicating ports, type of plantation and what it produced, for example, a sugar or coffee plantation.

A search of the RGS catalogue reveals a number of map titles for each of the islands in the Caribbean. The RGS can advise on the availability of these maps.

Make sure you prepare for your first visit to the RGS. It is an important part of how you manage your time effectively. Your first visit should be about trying to familiarise yourself with what is available and how to gain access to the maps. You can also get information about using the Foyle Reading Room for study and research. The RGS has a new seventy-seat room, purpose-built to support family history researchers using the Society's collection.

Well-resourced archives do make provisions for informed attendants to be on hand to offer advice and assistance. It makes sense to prepare a list of questions so that you can get yourself orientated as quickly as possible. Your questions should be the ones that you are unable to get answers to on the Internet. If you have a detailed inquiry it is advisable to book an appointment with the reading room staff. But note that there is a charge to cover one-to-one help, research and detailed inquires.

For security, lockers are provided for personal belongings and items that cannot be brought into the reading room. You will also be required to have your photograph taken on registration. Readers are allowed to use laptop computers.

To register as a new reader you will need to provide identification such as a driving licence or passport. There is a charge for using the room and you should always check the price in advance, on their website or by calling the RGS.

The National Libraries of the Caribbean

Finding out as much as you can about where your forebears settled is important in piecing together family history mysteries. National libraries are usually the source of some wonderful collections.

National libraries are responsible for collecting all publications issued in their respective countries. They also collect,

Case Study 7

I visited the Royal Geographical Society and obtained maps of Jamaica for 1798 and 1804. I had no idea that they existed. I had asked the attendant to simply show me what records he had of Jamaica. He assisted further by searching the card index and locating two noteworthy maps.

The maps were particularly interesting, made of beautifully dyed cloth and with fine original colour. The technique of making them demonstrated art and unbelievable accuracy in the registration of multiple colours on both sides of a single piece of material. The RGS holds large-scale maps that provide an astonishing level of detail about islands, towns and properties. The island of Jamaica is presented in some detail with the districts (precincts) clearly marked. I estimated that the maps were about two inches by four. The RGS were able to photocopy these maps, and to provide an A4 size map on paper. Some show the names of existing towns. I spotted Crooks' Cove Sugar Plantation at Cousins Cove, the place of my ancestral origins in Jamaica. When I compared the two maps I could see where changes in ownership had occurred.

The records at the family history centre revealed that my great-great-grandfather and his family lived at a place called Jerusalem Mountain. The national library of Jamaica, which also holds maps, had been unable to confirm the existence of such a place. However, the plantation maps (copies of which I obtained from the Royal Geographical Society) confirmed its existence over the border between Hanover and Westmoreland in 1804.

I discovered old maps of Caribbean islands containing the location and names of property and their owners.

preserve, document and facilitate access to the nation's cultural heritage. Many have not yet automated all records for their earlier acquisitions.

The computerised catalogue of books and pamphlets may be available online in the library. There may also be a computerised database of the map collection and card catalogues of Estate and Cadastral Maps, as it is with the National Library of Jamaica.

The National Library of Jamaica, for example, contains roughly 20,000 items, most of them in manuscript form. It includes land holdings of all sizes from both rural and urban settlements, including the layout of large estates, plantations and cattle pens.

The collections are not as complete for Barbados and the Leeward Islands where only a handful of plans are said to have survived. According to B.W. Higman, the situation is better for the Windward Islands and Guyana. Most of the plans for these territories can be found in European collections.

The maps at the National Library of Jamaica are particularly worthy of mention. A lot of the land was surveyed and sits with correspondence, indentures and printed advertisements. Reasons for the existence and survival of this material can be explained. Sugar plantations were large expanses of land which made them easy to map. During the 1700s and early 1800s, the high proportion of property owners (usually people of European descent) migrated back to the lands of their ancestors in Britain. They would have been relatively well-off individuals.

The popularity of mapping estates ensured the creation of large stocks of maps and surveys. Frequent boundary disputes required fresh surveys to be carried out more often than not. But there was one individual, Thomas Harrison, who – in keeping with Jamaica's strong tradition of record-keeping and archive preservation – made it his business to collect as many plans as he could in the late 1850s. His collection provides a useful resource if you are interested in locating family settlements that may once have existed.

The National Archives, London
The National Archives, Kew, London maintain documents and other materials relating to the activities of the British government

Case Study 8

The National Library of Jamaica (NLJ) kept property surveys dating back to slavery. I emailed the NLJ a request for information of surveys relating to Cousins Cove. I sent a postal order which cost a relatively small sum of money. I would also call occasionally to track my order. The staff were extremely helpful. Within two months I received a copy of a map dating back to 1820 and a report that included detailed information about the proprietors, Richard and William Dickson. From the survey map I identified two things of interest:

1. The location of the great house on the hill.
2. The slave village.

With further research, I found out that slaves used to bury their dead in the kitchen gardens, a practice which continued when slavery ceased. The shallow graves had been a mass burial ground.

The property was a sugar plantation with a mill. I observed the link between the plantation names and the names I had noticed in the baptism records. Some of the plantation names have survived to this day. It dawned on me that many of the towns in the Caribbean Islands are named after plantation owners who owned the town and acres of land around it.

With the 1820 survey of the Cousins Cove property, supplied to me by the National Library of Jamaica, in my hand and a good knowledge of how plantations were laid out, having read B.W. Higman,[11] I was able to locate the so-called 'great house' on the hill. I located fragments from the house and the slave village site. I knew that somewhere, on the acreage of land, was the burial place of my great-great-great-great-grandmother who died in 1825 on the Cousins Cove estate.

at home and abroad. Scholars and family historians make frequent use of the archives to write history. It is home to a wonderful collection comprising the records of the central government and law courts from the Domesday Book in 1086 to the present century. It also hosts an amazing collection of information related to the Caribbean Islands. Britain kept exceptional records on the lands under her control. These records are of interest to history writers including family historians. The records of the colonial office have been particularly important in this regard.

The slave registers

The estate records of the plantation owners are usually held in private collections. Those of smaller holdings are usually very difficult to track down. Perhaps the most consistent, accessible and important for people with African and/or European ancestors are all estate records of the slave registers stored at the National Archives.

The slave registers are the result of a plan to police the smuggling of slaves throughout the islands of the Caribbean. Its architect was James Stephen, the son of a supercargo (an officer on a merchant ship in charge of the cargo and its sale and purchase) who had been a lawyer in St Kitts in the Caribbean. He also succeeded Thomas Clarkson in the abolition movement.

According to the Jamaican historian Richard Hart: 'Surprised and annoyed to learn that slaves were being smuggled into the British West Indies, the House of Commons resolved in June 1810 that early in the next session they would consider measures to be adopted to prevent the violation of the law.' [12]

The law Hart was referring to related to the bill which declared the trafficking of Africans from the continent to the Caribbean illegal.

Hart also informs us that: 'The plan designed to facilitate detection and release of smuggled slaves was devised by James Stephen. He proposed that in each colony, a register of existing slaves be prepared on the basis of returns which the slave owners were to be required to make within a limited time. Thereafter, no slave was to be bought or sold without production of a registration certificate. Slave owners were to be further required to make periodical returns accounting for any increase or decrease by birth, purchase or death.'[13]

The registers were introduced in Trinidad as an experiment. In 1815, the registration was extended to St Lucia and Mauritius. If you are the descendent of Africans brought to the Caribbean and held in bondage, then the slave registers are your best hope of tracing those born prior to 1834. These registers can mark the beginning or the end of a line of inquiry in a search for an African ancestor and their origins on the continent. The registers will be of particular interest if you have European ancestors who were landowners or proprietors, overseers or attorneys to sugar estates and/or coffee plantations. This is what makes them potentially the most exciting of all public records for African and European researchers alike.

The amount of detail contained in the register varies from island to island. The Jamaican records are amongst the best in terms of the level of detail and consistency.

Description of Information Contained in Slave Registers	
Old name of slave	Normally nicknames (pet names – a Scottish term which reached Jamaica as a result of the ways of Scots who settled the island) or the names by which they were normally known. Dicky, Braveboy, Samson, Cambridge, Sambo, Billy Mary, Hilda, Pheobe, to name a few. Some Africans retained their birth names, such as, Quaco, Quamina, Beniba, Cudjoe, Sabba.
Christian name of slave	By 1817, almost all were African in origin or have African ancestors. These names may not have been in everyday use on the plantations.
Age of slave	The age of an African was usually assessed by an experienced doctor at the point of embarkation from Africa. They would look at teeth, assess bone structure and skin tone inter alia.
Remarks about the slave	Usually indicating the mother of the Creole. The column was left blank for Africans.

Description of Information Contained in Slave Registers	
African or Creole	Used to identify persons born on the island or originally from the African continent. 'Creole' entries had African ancestors that had embarked from ports along the West Coast of Africa any time prior to 1817 (usually before 1808 when the abolition of the transatlantic slave trade came into effect). The majority of 'Africans' included in registers are likely to have embarked from West Africa between 1775 and 1808.
Category to indicate miscegenation	Derived from the Latin words *miscere* (to mix) and *genus* (race), the term itself was coined in 1864 by David G. Croly and George Wakeman in their pamphlet *Miscegenation: The Theory of the Blending of the Races Applied to the American White Man and Negro*. The offspring of white-black unions in the Americas were categorised according to the number of generations they were removed from their African forebears. The rationale being that anyone classified as octoroon was legally white.

Sambo   child of mulatto and negro.
Mulatto   child of white man and negress.
Quadroon   child of mulatto woman and white man.
Mustee   child of quadroon [or pure Amerindian].
Mustiphini   child of mustee and white man.
Quintroon   child of mustiphini and white man.
Octoroon   child of quintroon and white man.

Why is the system of classification important in terms of African and European ancestral research? Understanding the classifications betrays the roots of negative attitudes towards Africans with dark skins still prevalent within 'black' and 'mixed-heritage/black' communities – and elsewhere. Debate about the system can invoke strong feelings of anger and outrage where informed individuals are concerned. It is a subject outside the scope of this book. Putting emotions to one side, these classifications are extremely useful in helping to verify the relationships of one person to another. For example, you might find several people with the same name, similar ages and born at the same place. You might be looking for somebody, and find that the father of your ancestor was classified as sambo. It means that one of the parents you are looking for would be classified as negro (African/black) and the other would be classified as mulatto (mixed-heritage/black). The classifications might be the only way of distinguishing between named slaves to find the one you're looking for.

Description of Information Contained in Slave Registers	
Attorney or overseer	Some of the children will have taken on the European surnames of individuals not listed as landowners or proprietors but employed in some other capacity (attorney, bookkeeper or indenture). Sometimes the owner's name is indicated on the register. Sometimes an estate was sold or left to a person and the name of an estate would change. Where an estate was left to a person it was usual for an executive to be appointed. It may be possible to find letters in the National Archives within the probate records.
The total number of slaves	The size of the community, which was also reflective of the size of many of the free villages and hamlets post-emancipation.
The number of males	
The number of females	
The proprietor	Usually wealthy European ancestry. Where the owner was absent (had returned to Europe), the name of the attorney would be indicated on the register.
Reason for addition to the register	Additions usually a result of a birth or hiring of an individual from another property.
Reason for deletion from the register	Deletion was usually because somebody had died during the period since the last register. It could also be because an individual was hired out to another property or worse sent to the workhouse for some misdemeanour.

The three-yearly updates to the 1817 slave registers

The 1817 slave registers were effectively a census indicating the names given to every slave known to be registered with a slave owner at a particular place and a given date. The registers were required to be updated every three years after 1817. The updates detail the reason for any increase or decrease in the number of slaves on a given plantation.

Increases resulting from the birth of individuals included the following information:

* The name of the child;
* Age at the time the register was taken;
* The colour classification;
* The mother of the child (who would not necessarily be a slave and therefore recorded on the 1817 register).

Decreases resulting from the death of an individual included the following information:

* Name of the individual;
* Age at the time the register was taken;
* Cause of death (it depended on the plantation owner as to whether this was recorded).

If there was another reason for a variation to the slave register, it would be indicated. Examples included Africans hired or sold to other plantations.

An extract from the 1826 register

Number of slaves on the 28th day of June 1826 - One Hundred and Seventy Five. Births since the last return, thirteen, deaths since the last return, twenty nine.

I, John Lee, attorney to Neil McCallum do swear that the above list and return is a true, perfect and complete list and return to the best of my knowledge and belief in every particular therein mentioned, of all and every slave and slaves... by me as attorney to Neil McCallum. Mortgage in professions consider it as most permanently settled, worked, or employed in the parish of Hanover on the twenty eighth day of June in the year of our Lord one thousand eight hundred and twenty six without fraud, deceit or evasion.

Sworn before me this first day of September 1826

Alex Grant

So help me God

John Lee attorney to Neil McCallum

Case Study 9

The baptism records for the parish of Hanover, 1834, recorded the name of my great-great-grandfather, William Crooks, and his siblings. They were all baptised on the same day eight years after the birth of the eldest. Also included is the name of their parents, my great-great-great-grandparents, John Alexander Crooks and Sarah Brown. The baptism records are evidence that they lived on the Cousins Cove Sugar Plantation. When I cross-referenced this with the slave registers of 1817, I found John Crooks, listed as negro African. I found no record of Sarah Brown. I wondered why?

Further investigation revealed that her name appeared in the updates to the 1817 slave register, documents which were tri-annually updated. I then linked Sarah Crooks to the children named in the baptism record. Interestingly, all of her children had been colour-classified as sambo. It was clear from the record that Sarah Brown was indeed of mixed heritage. Her exclusion from the 1817 slave register and references made about her in the subsequent updates as the mother of slave children, could be explained by her having been manumitted – set free.

Knowledge of those societies, uniquely structured around colour stratification helped me use the archives and repositories to discover my African slave ancestors. There were three John Crooks listed in records for the plantation on which John Alexander Crooks worked. My great-great-great-grandfather was classified as negro. One of the others was classified as a mulatto; the other, another racial mix. When the records revealed to me the racial mix of my great-great-grandfather, William Crooks, it was possible for me to verify which of the three men named John Crooks was my ancestor. For it was clear that only one could fit the profile.

There were a small number of slaves who are documented as having bought their freedom before acquiring other slaves. Being illiterate they would have signed their registers with an X in the middle or beside their name.

Researching the business relationships plantation owners may have had with slave traders could be interesting. Plantation owners may have even been slave traders themselves. Pursuit of this information may reveal connections with trade routes back to Africa and potentially the relationship between Africans and their descendants in the Caribbean and West Africa. It is absolutely essential to do this in conjunction with reading the books written about the slave trade[14] and the history of West Africa.

Compensation registers

Legislation was passed to abolish slavery in 1833. The legislation required Africans and African Creoles to enter a period of apprenticeship with their owner. This period was intended to last six years until 1840. The British justified this by the belief that Africans required time to learn the responsibilities that went with freedom. The reality was that slavery continued in all its manifestations. The ex-slave masters were handsomely compensated for letting go decades of institution.

Many African and African Creoles walked into the wilderness with only the clothes on their backs, a few small possessions and memories they would eventually dispose of, to begin life anew. Referring to the consequence of the legislation to emancipate Africans, Richard Hart says:

… only the system of exploiting labor was altered. Property relationships were not disturbed. The planters continued to own the plantations and, in addition, these former slave owners… received from the British government £20 million sterling compensation. But those who had been slaves, and therefore propertyless, before the transition remained propertyless and uncompensated after it. They entered the historic stage as free men but so divorced from ownership of property capable of producing wealth, that 150 years later the great majority of their descendents have known only persistent poverty.[15]

Asian immigration

Following emancipation in 1838, the British government introduced indentured servants from China and India to do the work that Africans were no longer willing to do without payment. A list of Asian immigrants to the islands can be found at the National Archives in the colonial office immigration records.

The National Archives holds British colonial records of former colonies Antigua, Bahamas, Barbados, Bermuda, Cayman Islands, Dominica, Grenada, Jamaica, Montserrat, Nevis, St Christopher (St Kitts), St Lucia, St Vincent, Tobago, Trinidad, Turks and Caicos Islands, and the British Virgin Islands, together with Guyana (formerly British Guiana), Belize (formerly British Honduras), and Sierra Leone, which administered many of the territories on the West Coast of Africa, because of the importance of West Africa in the history, people and development of the West Indies. The National Archives publication *Tracing Your West Indian Ancestors* by Guy Grannum describes the records and includes reference numbers which you would need to quote in order to access National Archive material.

If you've managed to locate the estate linking you to your forebears, the chances are that there will be a compensation claim related to that property. Absentee owners would have appointed attorneys to continue productive activity on plantations. Compensation claims may indicate the number of slaves, the type of skills they had and the work they performed. Property owners received more compensation for skilled labourers than they did for field labourers. They received nothing for slaves with a disability. Some owners made separate claims for children born between 1832 and 1834. The National Archives retain records of appeals against proposed compensation payments. Again, the level of detail contained within may vary from parish to parish and island to island.

The majority of indigenous British people have connections with the slave trade. The further back they go, the more likely the connection would be to a slave plantation in the Caribbean. In his book *Capitalism and Slavery*, Eric Williams provides a fascinating insight into the contribution of the West Indian planter, aided by the African workforce, to the growth of Britain up to and throughout the Industrial Revolution. Plantations were increasing in size and profitability from the mid eighteenth century onwards. The years from 1764 to 1804 would have been a boom period within the colonies in terms of the wealth Europeans had been accumulating from the triangular trade; this was the period when the population of capitalists and small-time entrepreneurs of Liverpool, Bristol, Manchester and London would have exploded as a direct consequence of finance from wealthy West Indian planters.

'Many a humble individual in England rose to wealth and affluence from some chance legacy of a West Indian plantation. The time came when such a legacy was considered gall and wormwood, but it was not so in the eighteenth century. George Colman's play, "Africans", portrays in young Mr Marrowbone, the butcher, a situation that must have been very familiar to the audience. The butcher was left a West Indian plantation, and "now barters for blacks, instead of bargaining for bullocks".'[16]

Indigenous Britons researching their ancestry may find an ancestor inherited large amounts of money during the seventeenth and eighteenth centuries and early parts of the nineteenth century. The possibility of ancestral involvement in the slave trade may well explain this. It is to the Caribbean the reader should look to seek the answer. Wills and probate records would be an important source of information to pursue this. People of British descent born on the islands (Creoles) may have willed money to relatives in England.

Case Study 10

I was surprised going through the compensation registers to find that in 1833 a separate claim had been submitted for children under the age of two years old living on the Cousins Cove Sugar Plantation. My great-great-grandfather, William Crooks was included in that claim. The entry indicated that he was one year and seven months old at the time of the claim. This was verified by an entry I found in the 1834 baptism records, the same record that confirmed that his father John Alexander Crooks had been a labourer.

Registers of passenger lists
The records of the Board of Trade are useful for tracing immigrants. It was a legal requirement for passenger lists to be submitted to port officers of the Ministry of Transport and sent to the Board of Trade. Its main use was for compiling statistics.

The lists are arranged under the names of the ports of arrival. They are of limited use, and may only be helpful if the name of the ship is already known. This makes it doubly important to talk to friends of the family who knew others who would have known or may have travelled on the same ship as the person you are seeking information about.

The entries are not always complete and there are omissions for a few ports. Complete records are informative and have the potential to open unexpected lines of inquiry.

The passenger records can confirm:

* Date of birth. The exact date of birth could be decisive in determining whether you would be able to find a birth certificate at the family history centre, if one exists. This is useful if you intend to search back through the generations;
* Address at which Caribbean immigrants resided after disembarking at British ports;

Case Study 11

My father told me that when he came to England at the age of seventeen, he went to live in Hackney, London. He had an address to go to but no idea how to get there. When he arrived, the lady who answered the door did not know who he was. That was until he identified himself as the son of her favourite uncle.

He said he left Kingston and arrived at Southampton. My father referred to his passport which he had kept. It had been stamped 19 October 1957. At first I thought this was the date he arrived. The passenger records at the National Archives would confirm that it was the date he left Jamaica. The records confirm his arrival in England on 3 November 1957 aged eighteen. The list for the *Irpinia* shows that it was a great carrier of Caribbean migrants, 507 in all. I wondered about friendships that were made on the journey. I imagine many of these friendships would have ceased soon after these individuals disembarked at Southampton and made their way to addresses located throughout Britain's main conurbations. The *Irpinia* carried people that had settled in places such as Birmingham, Bristol, Huddersfield, Manchester, Cardiff, Nottingham, Sheffield, Northampton and other places. I had less success finding a comparable list for my mother who arrived in the United Kingdom by air during the early sixties.

* Skills or jobs (electricians, welders, mechanics, fishermen dressmakers, labourers and cultivators);
* Country of origin or last permanent residence;
* Individual marital status on arriving in Britain. This could provide a useful indicator for locating marriage dates and certificates which, as already mentioned, can provide a wealth of information to unlock doors to previous generations. The younger they are the more chance you have of narrowing down the possible year of marriage.

Other information includes:

* Class of travel;
* Port of embarkation;
* Sex;
* Adults of twelve years and over;
* Children aged between one and twelve;
* Infants under one year;
* Citizenship;
* Total numbers travelling.

Preparing for your visit to the National Archives
The National Archives, like many of the large public records facilities, is constantly innovating and improving its systems to support speedier access to public records. At the time of writing, public records systems seem to be undergoing a major program of modernisation. More and more records are being digitised and being made available online, IT systems are constantly reviewed to make searching far more accessible for people, particularly the elderly who are not used to using computers. Standards for waiting times have been introduced to ensure that you do not have to wait too long for your records to arrive from the minute you have placed your order. Again, like other large public records institutions, customer service support for people who are not quite sure where to begin or how to use systems is also of a high quality.

Familiarise yourself with the layout of the facility and how records are arranged and accessed. Do this before making a serious effort to uncover information. It will help you to make the most efficient use of your time in subsequent visits and reduce the 'false starts' in the long run. A reader's ticket must be obtained to view original records. These are issued as soon as you can provide adequate means of identification They help you to accomplish most things during a visit such as placing your order and checking where it is in the system, even when you are somewhere else in the building perhaps having a coffee.

The National Archives have a range of leaflets and Internet information to help you prepare in advance so that you do not waste time. Records are divided into 'classes', which have names and unique identifiers. You must know the complete reference numbers for anything that you order.

Many of the documents you will see and may want to copy are fragile. So it is worth finding out where the photocopying facilities are, and approaching one of the attendants and have them explain rules about usage and handling documents. This ensures that the records are preserved for future generations of family historians.

Monumental Inscriptions

Monumental inscriptions mark the place where the dead are laid to rest. In the Caribbean Islands, only the affluent had their resting place marked with a tombstone; a handful compared to the total population at any given time. Poor people in rural areas buried their dead in kitchen gardens. Few tombstones, if any, would be maintained if they were buried outside the church burial grounds.

Finding the name and date of birth and date of death inscribed on a tombstone is about as much as one can hope for. Monumental inscriptions in some of the Caribbean islands are recorded by people with an interest in their Caribbean ancestry. They can be useful if you are trying to identify the burial places of affluent European Caribbean people. It is only in recent times that people with African ancestors have been buried in church burial grounds.

For some, a walk in the churchyard cemetery may be a ghoulish experience. For others, visiting the last resting place of ancestors on a warm summer's day to read inscriptions can feel quite pleasurable.

Salt blowing in from the Caribbean Sea is known to have a weathering effect on the old tombstones. If you find evidence of

Case Study 12

At the time when I discovered the monumental inscriptions for Jamaica, I was aware that there may have been some connection with the parish of Hanover. I wondered whether there was a sugar plantation owned by the person from whom the family name originated.

A search revealed the name James Crooks buried in Lucea. There were no other Crookses listed. I deduced that James Crooks was most certainly affluent and likely to have owned land in close proximity to the Hanover's main business centre. The trail had become hot! My assumptions would be confirmed during a later visit to the map reading room at the Royal Geographical Society.

a burial, visit the churchyard and take a camera with you. You may be able to obtain pictures of gravestones and monumental inscriptions to place amongst your archive documentation.

The Newspaper Library, London

Old newspapers can prove a useful source when building a picture of life during a certain period. Serving as a daily log, they depict the political, social, technological, economic and culture environment at a given place and time.

The Colindale Newspaper Library based in north-west London, is a branch of the British Library. The library holds perhaps the most important collection of newspapers relating to lands controlled by the British government. Most of the newspapers are held on microfilm. The library maintains a collection of the world's important historic newspapers including collections from Caribbean islands. Past copies of local, national and international newspapers are available.

So how can newspapers help you? The newspapers of the Caribbean were concerned with international, national and state affairs. There was a particular emphasis on business and trade.

The newspaper library is a particularly rich source of information if you're looking to link a European surname to a geographic location and associated business interest.

Announcements of births, marriages, divorces and deaths can be found in the personal columns. Naturally this normally relates to wealthy European families. The announcements contain references to other members of the family and other connected individuals. Use this information source to add to what you already know. They may help to confirm stories that have come down through the generations.

Newspapers provide limited information about the circumstances of direct African and Asian ancestors. A striking feature of Caribbean newspapers is the large sections devoted to notices of sales of Africans and other commodities: notices of auctions provide information unobtainable anywhere else. Notices of ships arriving with a 'cargo' of Africans, announcements of sales of slaves and notices of runaways littered newspapers; such notices included the names and sometimes a description of the runaways. It is interesting that British local newspapers printed during the 1800s reported on poor people, often black people, on the streets of London, who had been arrested for some minor misdemeanour, such as drunkenness, and other poverty-related issues. The Greenwich Archives in London is one example of a local archive that has retained newspaper cuttings recording names of individuals and their hardships. They make for an interesting and informative read about the lives of poor people in Britain, which included many Africans among the street homeless.

The proliferation of notices within Caribbean newspapers relating to runaway slaves during the late 1700s to early 1800s coincided with the masters' concern for their own safety in the colonies, as slave resistance began to increase in its many forms. Notices of runaways made references to Africans as Moco, Congo, Mundingo and Coromantees, possibly indicating their origins. These were times when the African population had grown to such an extent that the Europeans found it overwhelming. All this at a time when property owners were increasingly concerned about the viability of their businesses in the face of the threat of cheap sugar production from within the French colonies. Many property owners opted to return to the places in Europe they regarded as their motherlands.

There were also notices of Africans taken from specific states along the west coast of Africa – from places as far south as Angola.

Advertisements were prominent in the front page of the Jamaican *Royal Gazette*. By modern standards the layout could easily have been mistaken for an advertising spread. The names of ships sailing from London's Liverpool were also listed.

Depending on the period, sections in some papers provide information about locals involved in various trading activities. For example, the *Royal Gazette*, Saturday, 29 July 1809, lists people with properties within the parish of St Elizabeth who, for whatever reason, had not provided a list of land, slaves and stock in their possession to the magistrates and vestry by the 20th of June. There are numerous property owners of European origin named and shamed. Lists like this are important because it is possible to trace towns and settlements named after some of these individuals. If your family came from a hamlet, town or village within a parish ostensibly named after a person, it may be possible to trace information about that person and property. The information you find may reveal historic connections between the property, the owner and your family name. With this information, it may be possible to get closer to identifying names of original settlements and plantations (refer to the section on the Royal Geographical Society to identify maps). The information may possibly lead you to linking names and properties to merchants and slave ship owners. Ships invariably sailed from Britain to Africa and then on to the Americas before heading home (refer to section on slave ships).

Remember ownership would have changed over time along with the names of the owners and attorneys. The newspapers can supplement your search by helping you identify a wide range of surnames linked to properties in the parish, not just owners; names of places that may not have been indicated on maps or slave registers where you suspect your forebears laboured.

There are other types of listings within old newspapers; for example, the monthly-produced lists of jurors for each of the parishes. The people included in these lists were esteemed whites: churchwardens, property owners or merchants. If you are looking for a surname common across an island or parish, then there is a possibility that by perusing the list of jurors, you may be able to link the surname to a large plantation. The next step would be to look in the National Archives for records of the property. The slave register will certainly reveal the name of the property owner. If you're interested in finding out more details about the proprietor and his associates, then you may find the list of jurors in the local newspaper worth investigating.

Admission to the newspaper library is free. A reader's ticket is relatively easy to obtain. Passes are issued to applicants in person within the newspaper reading rooms. Make sure you bring proof of identity. Check on the Internet to see their requirements.

You should arrive early if you have never used the facilities. Allow yourself enough time to identify microfilms, newspapers and anything else of interest. Microfilms for Caribbean newspapers are in storage. If you haven't placed your order online, then use the catalogues available at the library to look up items of interest, before placing your order.

You can order up to four items by phone, fax, email or letter.[17] Advance requests must be received a minimum of forty-eight hours (excluding Sundays) before the date required. When ordering, you must state:

* Your name;
* The title and date of the newspaper or journal you wish to request;

* The date you require the items;
* For overseas titles only, you must also state the shelf mark, your telephone, fax or email contact details so that they can advise you if any of the items you have requested are unavailable.

The library advises that you telephone or email in advance of your visit, in order to ascertain that it does hold the information you require and, if so, to reserve it so that it is available on your arrival.

Orders are made on slips, which you would present to the counter. It can take up to forty minutes to receive your order. Microfilm readers take some time getting used to, and time can go very quickly – especially if you are particularly excited by the possibilities of what you might discover. You may not understand how to use microfilm readers even after being shown once. There isn't time to waste; if you're not sure, don't hesitate to ask the attendant for help. Do so until you're satisfied that you can operate the readers.

India Office records collection

The administration in London kept documentary archives for the India Office records. The records cover the period 1600 to 1947, and comprise masses of volumes of official publications, manuscripts and maps. There are a number of records that show how the indentured labour system was run and which reveal the political and social problems it provoked. This can be found in the departmental records series. It includes letters between administrators in India and London, copies of letters that circulated between administrators in India, official and unofficial reports, subject files and newspaper cuttings. Most documentation was created by British administrators and therefore presents the British, rather than the Indian, point of view.[18]

A health officer's report of 1858 lists the births and deaths on a

Case Study 13

It was curiosity that drove me to take my first visit to the Colindale News-paper Library. I had no real expectations. The choice of newspapers for Jamaica was surprisingly limited. I had perhaps an unrealistic expectation that the library had archived all Jamaican newspapers going back to the first contact Britain had with the Caribbean Islands. I was somewhat comforted by the fact that there wasn't so much to choose from, and if there was nothing to find then I would know sooner rather than later.

I was disappointed to find that the Jamaican newspapers at the Colin-dale Library contained very little information about specific local activities in each of the parishes. However, I was extremely surprised to see a notice that John Crooks of the Crooks Cove Sugar Plantation was looking for slaves who had run away. The notice was dated 1791. It confirmed that there was a John Crooks, from whom my great-great-great-grandfather took his name. It confirmed that the Crooks Cove Sugar Plantation took its name from that of the owner. As I had suspected.

I became curious about the set of films which related to the emancipa-tion. Here I found the notice of compensation that was paid to plantation owners for setting slaves free. In the batch of films that related to the pre-war period, notices of runaway slaves and the imported Africans were replaced by adverts for medicines, foods and clothing. It made me think about the picture on my wall of my grandfather, and how these adverts would have influenced the way he dressed and what he ate. It also made me think about how easy it was for the colonial masters to offload sur-pluses at great profit; and when slavery ended, how the door opened for Europeans to take advantage of markets that previously did not exist.

ship bringing Indians to Demerara.[19] A 1914 Government of India report gives detailed information on the housing, wages, health and diet of Indian immigrants in Trinidad. A 1939 Colonial Office report describes labour conditions throughout the West Indies. In describing the position of Indians, the administrators naturally had to explain the larger context, and this makes the records a valuable source for Caribbean studies generally.

The short-lived nature of newspapers means that there is a limit to what is available. For this reason, it is better to be clear about what you want to get from the records. Try narrowing your search to a specific geographical area and a specific year. This will prepare you for your visit to the library. There is an inquiry desk where the library staff would be able to help answer your queries.

An outline of the main record classes, with lists of some individual files, is contained in Timothy N. Thomas's *Indians Overseas: A Guide to Source Materials in the India Office Records for the Study of Indian Emigration 1830–1950.*

The National Maritime Records

Slave ship records may be useful if you are at the end stage of your search. It is unlikely that you will find the name of an African ancestor from any of the records of British slave ships that embarked from Africa; unless the captain or some other crew member retained personal records that have been preserved down through the ages. The records that survive today for British slave ships do not contain the names of Africans that were put on board.

Scholars have published the Trans-Atlantic Slave Trade Database on CD-ROM[20] from the major primary sources of information about trade routes around the world. These authors have put together the largest compilation of raw data ever made regarding the shipment of slaves from Africa to the Americas between 1588 and 1867. They claim to have compiled records of 27,233 slave trips to the New World, or seventy per cent of all voyages made between 1595 and 1866 from all over Europe. Also, they have compiled ninety per cent of all voyages from British ports. Note that these ships left with the intention of completing a triangular journey that took them to Africa to the Americas and back to

Case Study 14

I discovered from the 1817 slave registers that the owners of the Cousins Cove estate were Richard Dickson and his son William.

The National Library of Jamaica provided information in a report of an estate survey conducted in 1821. The report indicated that there was a John Dickson who was the named owner of an adjacent property. I came across a newspaper article indicating that they had property further afield in another parish. It also gave the name of his son, William Dickson, a militiaman. A search of the newspaper library revealed that he served as a juror and that he was also a merchant. British merchants trading with the West Indies, without exception, were involved in the lucrative trafficking of Africans.

I subsequently discovered that a slave ship, *The Schooner James*, reached the shores of Jamaica in 1798. The ship had been owned by William Dickson.

When I realised the existence of the Trans-Atlantic Slave Trade Database I decided to put it to the test, hoping that it would reveal information, perhaps the names of individual Africans. Sadly it did not. I was however surprised that it did contain further details about William Dickson's exploits.

The Schooner James had embarked from West Africa on five occasions, between 1798 and 1799. It transported Africans purchased from ports at Calabar and New Calabar, from the coastal area known as Bight of Biafra. The schooner disembarked at Jamaica on each occasion. For one of those journeys the CD revealed, amongst other things, National Archives reference numbers: C0140/89,369; BT98/59,345; BT98/58,167); and *Lloyd's List* publications in March, January and April, 1798. I felt certain that my great-great-great-grandfather John Alexander Crooks was a captive on the schooner during one of those trans-Atlantic crossings.

I wondered about the source of all this information. The CD had a section on documentary sources identified in public records in Portugal, Brazil, United States of America, Denmark and of course Great Britain. In Great Britain, extensive research had been undertaken at more obvious places such as the British Library, National Archives and the National Maritime Museum. Less obvious was the fact that institutions such as the Bank of England and prominent universities were also rich sources of information.

Slave ports were clustered along the coast of West Africa from Senegal's Fort Saint Louis to ports along Angola in West-Central Africa. Between 1776 and 1800, a quarter of the Africans (315,000) that were transported by British ships to the Americas came from the Bight of Biafra, the region we know today as Nigeria. The main anchorages were at New Calabar, Bonny and Old Calabar. Almost twenty per cent (200,000) had been transported from the Bight of Benin, which would have included the regions along the west coast known today as Togo and Benin. Approximately fifteen per cent (180,000) would have been transported from Cape Coast Castle on the Gold Coast, present-day Ghana. People identified in the slave registers as Africans are likely to have been transported from these important zones.

It seemed reasonable to deduce that there was a direct, and possibly long-standing, business relationship between the proprietor of Crooks Cove (John Crooks) and his neighbours the Dicksons who established ownership of the Cousins Cove Sugar plantation sometime after 1804 and before 1812.

England. An important source of information is the shipping paper of the eighteenth and nineteenth centuries, the *Lloyd's List*, which can be found – as for most of British history – preserved at the National Archives in London. The *Lloyd's List* is the most comprehensive information source on shipping movements during the eighteenth century. Slave ships of every nationality are contained within the *Lloyd's List*, and it is maintained even to the present day. From 1747, the British government required masters or owners of merchant ships to maintain details of ship voyages. The details or musters are found within the National Archives Board of Trade papers BT 98.

The database contains information on ship construction and registration and an extensive record of owners' and captains' names. This may be useful to Europeans, North Americans and Africans tracing their connections with Africa and the trafficking of Africans.

Africans with Caribbean ancestry seeking to find their African roots are commonly concerned to find out whether the names of slaves were listed. The scholars have researched this, and revealed that only in Latin America was it not unusual to list the names of slaves. They say that most African historians have had to rely on Latin American records in order to identify their origins on the African continent. In North American records this was less common. As indicated in the previous chapter African names that remained unchanged after the journey though the Middle Passage may have been recorded in the 1817 slave registers. Africans who were forced to board slave ships assumed the status of cargo. Like cargo, only the quantity of 'raw materials used for slaving purposes' was recorded. The authors acknowledge that the data can only be used indirectly to locate the African origins of groups of slaves arriving in America at a given time and a given place.

Locating a copy of the database CD for purchase requires high levels of persistence and determination. If you manage to get a copy, then you might find it a prohibitively expensive source of information: more so, if you harbour real doubts about where your ancestors embarked or disembarked from in West Africa, England and the Caribbean.

The CD package is designed with educators and students of Africa and the African diaspora in mind. It is of very limited interest to most except the most determined diasporians tracing their roots. Europeans searching for connections to the triangular trade would probably gain more information from the database.

In Summary

Oral accounts help you to prepare the first draft of your family tree. When you have done this, you will be able to identify gaps in your information. This is the first step towards achieving clarity about the objectives you should be pursuing. As a minimum, you are looking for dates, places and names. Talk to close friends of the family if you do not know a recent forebear's date of birth. If they can tell you your forebear's island of origin, when they arrived in Britain and if it was on a ship, then you should be well placed to locate the ship's passenger lists which would reveal their date of birth.

The next step is to search for family history centres run by the Church of the Latter-day Saints. There you will find birth, baptism, marriage and death records – your springboard to the past. They will contain names of your parents, where and when they lived and an indication as to what they did for a living. The further back you go, the closer you get to discovering African, African Creole, European, Asian and slave ancestors. You will also be able to find others connected with properties in the Caribbean. Identifying the parish where your forebears settled would ensure that you are well placed to find the precise location of the settlement using geographic records. If you have reason to believe that your name or settlement is connected to a wealthy or influential person, then publications will provide a vehicle for obtaining further clues. Eventually you will locate records within the National Archives at home and abroad. To reconstruct plantation life, you will need to undertake a search of literature and land surveys. When you've exhausted the sources and had a degree of success, you may find yourself in a position to realise the possibility of making links back to Africa.

The names of plantation owners may lead to merchants who navigated particular slave routes on the way to disembarking slaves in the Caribbean. If you have an ancestor that retained their African name, then it is possible to locate the region and possibly the village from which they originated!

Potential Pitfalls

Acquisition of new names and name changes
A step-by-step approach will guarantee that you succeed in tracing how you came by your surname.

African descendents in the Caribbean acquired European names through seasoning, whereby they were made to cast off their names, their culture and ideas of independence and personal development. A hybrid culture was born which was later added to when the East Indians and Chinese settled in the Caribbean Islands.

Literature will throw up many names connected with the Caribbean Islands. History books and television documentaries often make reference to Europeans who had strong connections with the Caribbean. Many of these names live on, having been passed from plantation owners to slaves and indentured servants through to the present-day descendants of the Africans of the Caribbean. Go straight to the index of some of the non-fictional books about the Caribbean to find an abundance of European names. It should not be too difficult to recognise and associate some unusual or less common names of African Caribbean families known to you.

Eric Williams's *Capitalism and Slavery* makes reference to the following names connected with the Caribbean:

Attwood	Carlyle	Francis	Gregson	Lecky
Auckland	Clapham	Francklyn	Gurney	Long
Baillie	Cobbett	Garbett	Hamilton	Luaber
Beckford	Codrington	Gascoyne	Harlow	Mantoux
Blundell	Cowper	Gaston-	Heywood	Marryat
Bolton	Cropper	Martin	Hibbert	McDowall
Boulton	Davenport	Gee	Hume	Miles
Bright	Defoe	Gibson	Hutt	Mittleberger
Brougham	Edwards	Gladstone	Jeffreys	Monk
Burke	Ewart	Glassford	Knight	O'Connell
Burn	Fortescue	Goulburn	Lascelles	Okhill

Ortiz	Raynal	Sturge	Tucker	Whitney
Oswald	Ricardo	Sypher	Walpole	Wilkinson
Phillips	Roebuck	Tarleton	Warner	Williamson
Pinney	Roscoe	Thomson	Wedgwood	Winthorpe
Price	Saco	Thornton	Wertonbaker	
Ragatz	Southey	Touchet	Whitmore	

The more common your name, the better the chance of identifying a link to a European proprietor or property. However, it may be more of a challenge to verify the individual you are looking for. For example, you may find many unconnected families within the parish who share the same surname because their African ancestors underwent seasoning and adopted the name of a European proprietor or associate. It may make more sense to trace your lineage back through a parent or grandparent with a unique or uncommon surname. Your success rate may increase exponentially. It all depends on the objective you set yourself at the start of the process.

It is a common feature of Caribbean society for people to have pet names as well as Christian names. Close scrutiny of plantation records reveals that not all Africans from the continent and their descendants acquired Christian names and European surnames. Some will have come by their names willingly as part of their expressed desire to convert to Christianity. Others will have adopted European names because it was expedient. This practice is evident, even in modern times, where people are forced to seek refuge in other lands and change names to escape persecution.

Africans would have adopted names to secure work on other plantations post-emancipation. Association with a well-known planter could sometimes prove decisive in gaining employment, temporary or otherwise. Also, close scrutiny of plantation records reveals that some Africans from the continent and their children retained their African name.

Case Study 15

My great-great-great-great-grandmother managed to retain her African name. This made it possible to confirm her origins in West Africa. Her name, Ami Djaba, is specific to the Krobo people of the South Eastern region, Ghana. The Krobo's original home is on the Krobo Mountain which is in close proximity to the Volta region. Krobo people record the past by clan traditions. The ancestral home of the Djaba household was at Plau on Krobo Mountain.

When I discovered these, I felt the urge to visit Ghana and seek out other members of the clan.

As a result of my interaction with the Krobo people, I became hungry for knowledge of the history of the Krobo. I searched on the Internet and read books which led me to discover the following: Every Krobo belongs to three social units; a family tree unites a number of patrilineal kin groups. Not all will claim descent from the same ancestor under one name. The family tree may therefore be classed as a sub-tribe rather than a clan. The Krobo are also part of the smaller social units or clans. These members will descend from a common ancestor or from an immigrant kinsgroup. The names of people in these clans were frequently derived from the location of either their settlement on a particular place on the Krobo Mountain or the ancestral home, but usually not from the ancestral founder. In each clan there are a number of family groups (houses). Members of each house descend from a particular male line. The family or house would also be ruled by its most senior male.[21]

Finding your roots on the African continent

The name is the key to unlocking the mystery of your roots in Africa. If you are fortunate enough to have found an African related to you on that register, with their African name intact, then you should be thrilled; it would make it possible for you to trace your roots to a specific African nation or community.

To be able to complete your quest, it would be important to

take time to find out about the history of African settlements and the African pattern of social groupings in West Africa.

The same principles are likely to apply to other tribes, communities, nations or polities in West Africa. This is what makes it possible to connect an African name on a slave record to a particular village or community in West Africa.

Tales from the past

There are inherent difficulties with messages passed on by the spoken word. The memory can also be selective, which can explain why one relative's account of a particular event can differ from another's. So, you are unlikely to get a complete diary of events. There's also the risk that stories are embellished to make them entertaining. To get to the truth, you have to filter fact from fiction. It means that everything you hear must be verified where possible.

Each time an anecdote is repeated there is a risk that words or sentences are added. Even the slightest change could have a profound effect on the meaning of the message imparted. Personal descriptions can be misleading; for example, people referred to as 'aunts' and 'uncles' when in fact they were friends of the family. An individual's perspective of an event may differ from another person observing the same event. Weigh up the competing perspectives. Don't be too quick to discount one version of events by completely favoring another.

The brothers who came from afar to settle

A story often recounted by families from Jamaica, and possibly other parts of the Caribbean, is the story of the brothers – usually two or three – that came from Scotland to settle at a named place on some Caribbean island. There, they parted company, usually after an argument, to journey to other parts of the island and to spread the name across the island.

Case Study 16

I found a record of my great-grandfather Robert Crooks at the family history centre. It was a baptismal record, and it contained the name of his father and the place where they lived.

It took me several visits to decipher the place of birth. The writing was neat, but for me it was unintelligible. It was later that I discovered the word was Jerusalem – Jerusalem Mountain. How did I find this out? By perusing a map of Jamaican plantations I discovered a property by the name of Jerusalem on the border between two parishes. The contours indicated a place high in the hills or on top of a mountain.

The origin of physical characteristics

Some may claim Maroon ancestry on the basis of skin colour and sometimes a misinformed view about who the Maroons really were. This is rooted in the misguided belief that the Maroons were Indians with long straight hair and dark skin with a reddish tinge.

Family trees

You could have as many as four grandparents, eight great-grand-parents, sixteen great-great-grandparents and so on. And if one of your great-grandparents parented ten children, then the number of relatives you could be searching for could easily number into the thousands. It may be sensible to avoid an attempt to find every family member and every branch of the tree.

Human error

Old documents can help you uncover name changes. Those who settled the Caribbean after slavery from the 1840s onward may well have had a name change. This would be common if they spoke little or no English. A clerk creating a record may well have made decisions to simplify a name that they felt had been too complicated to spell. They may have spelled names phonetically, the way they were pronounced. This would have been true of Africans held in bondage on Caribbean islands. It would also have applied to Asians from the continent, settled in the Caribbean. There wasn't a correct way of spelling African names; and they would not have been asked to express their preferred spelling either.

After emancipation in 1838, many Africans in the diaspora were denied the benefits of a complete and structured education. They would have adopted European names, which many would not have known how to spell. Here again, the clerk would have had more power than they realised. Even with Christian names, discrepancies can be found within the records. Browne could change to Brown, Crooks could change to Crookes. Browne could easily have changed to Brooks. And such changes could then have been carried down the generations. Below are some different spellings of the same African name in order to illustrate the point.

FIRST NAME

Ashanti	Fanti	Jamaica	European translation
Kwadjo	Kojo	Cudjoe/Cudjo	Monday
Kwabena	Kobina	Cubina Cubbenah	Tuesday
Kwaku	Kweku	Quaco	Wednesday
Yaw	Ekow	Quao, Quaw Yaw, Quayhoo	Thursday
Kofi	Kofi	Cuffee Cophy Coffee	Friday
Kwame	Kwamina	Quamin	Saturday

Ashanti	Fanti	Jamaica	European translation
Kwasi	Kwesi	Quashie	Sunday

Parents may have altered their children's names at baptism; first names might have been dropped or reversed. It is common in Caribbean communities for pet names to be adopted. This practice dates back to the days of slavery (see section on slave registers).

Handwriting

Computer records (which rely on the input of entry clerks) may also contain human errors. Before the IT revolution, clerks would transcribe words from certificates to ledgers. A name written in one register could easily have been misread by the clerk. So, you are inevitably going to come across transcription errors. Also, documents can be difficult to read if they have been microfilmed. If you are reading from microfilm, then magnify the word. You may find that by looking at the words letter by letter you are able to work out the correct word.

Interpreting and Documenting Your Findings

Recording Interviews

If you prefer to use a recording device for interviewing purposes, make sure your recording device is positioned unobtrusively. You really do not want to cause your interviewee to clam up. Dictaphone devices can cause your interviewee to be over-conscious that they are being recorded and inhibit the flow of storytelling or conversation. Dictaphones have non-directional microphones, which means that they should be held close to the mouth in order to pick up a clear sound. When starting the interview, begin by recording five to ten minutes of general chatter. This will help your interviewee to feel relaxed. Maintain eye contact, only looking at your notebook to take notes. Always anticipate that tapes may run out, whilst your interviewee is in mid flow.

Do not underestimate how easy it is to overwrite recordings accidentally. When you have finished the interview, make sure you break the tab on the tape or recording media to prevent you overwriting conversations, then write up the taped conversation as soon as possible. There can be nothing worse than waiting until you've returned home from your vacation only to find gaps in your information. And if on playing back a tape you find your

Case Study 17

I discovered a record of William Crooks' marriage to Ellen in 1855. They were married in the parish of Westmoreland. I had assumed that this was where he was born. Yet I could find no birth or baptism record for him. I thought a further search of the parish might reveal his parents. I found records of three slaves who were baptised in the parish and whose surnames were Crooks. Two of them were female and the third was a male. I assumed they were linked to William in some way. Something nagged at me; I was never truly satisfied that I had found William's parents. So I kept on searching. I would eventually find his parents in the neighbouring parish, Hanover.

When I finally discovered my great-great-grandfather's, William Crooks, baptismal record, I was surprised to find he was baptised on the same day as his siblings in 1834. However, further scrutiny of the records revealed an entry for his mother, Sarah 'Brooks'. The same for his older sibling Barbary, who was recorded on the line above him. And on the line above Barbary was his older brother, John. His mother was recorded as Sarah Brown. The baptism record gave the ages: William, two years old; Barbary, four years old; and John, eight years old. Their father was John Crooks. Discovery of the slave registers of 1817 and the subsequent updates verified that Sarah Brown was the mother of three children.

recordings are poor quality then you are at the mercy of your ability to recall what you heard.

There is a danger of hearing what you want to hear – and not what is actually being said. Remain objective and open-minded and avoid emotional involvement.

Avoid distractions. Don't let your mind wander or be distracted by your interviewee's dress, or unconscious habits.

Active listening keeps you on your toes. Ask yourself what key point the interviewee is making? How does this fit with what other members of the family have told you?

Recording Information from Original Documentation

Difficulty reading documents can be frustrating. It may cause you to interpret words incorrectly. It is better to take copies of documentation away to be studied carefully, as the information will not always make sense on first reading. A lack of familiarity reading old-style writing may cause difficulty in deciphering certain words on the page. Try to familiarise yourself with the style of writing and letter formation by scanning over other words either side of the word you are having problems with, or sentences on the page containing similar letters. The key is to try and find other documentation that can verify your findings or any conclusions you may have reached.

Earlier chapters emphasise the need to prepare for visits to public records. Preparation is about making sure you get the most from your visit. Part of the process of familiarising yourself with the records involves checking with the attendants if it is possible to make photocopies of documents. You also need to find out which documents you are not permitted to photocopy.

The next step is to get down to the business of identifying key documents. The first thing to do when you locate a document you think is relevant is make a note of the information it contains including any file or document reference number, volume and page. A word of caution, sometimes the excitement of finding something of interest can – and often does – lead to hastily written notes. But writing notes can save you the trouble of rushing to the photocopier every minute. Save photocopying for later, just before you're ready to leave. You can go home and examine your discoveries at your leisure.

Presenting Information

The information you collect will grow. The pile of documents in the corner of your room should be a prompt to organise the documentation and information.

A computer-generated family tree can transform your sketch

or scribbles into an attractive centrepiece for your room. Family tree packages offer a range of designs to choose from; you can include photos, and multimedia trees are complete with audio and video clips. You can have your tree professionally handwritten and illustrated with your own personal, stylish touches. This type of service is often advertised in family history magazines. Consider packages that enable you to create notes about an individual or a marriage, and that store photographs and images.

If you're less inclined to produce it yourself, you can always try one of the many printing services specialising in printing large trees in both colour and black-and-white. You can search the Internet for contacts. Some will custom-design your charts, while others allow you to select from a number of different formats. Some may require you to send your tree in a database format.

A pleasurable way of bringing the past to life is to write your own family history in the form of a narrative. It is about recounting the story of the family's journey through time and across continents together with the historic milestones that helped shape their lives – and ultimately yours. Most of what we have now come to expect as the history of the Caribbean, comes from the accounts, perspectives and interpretation of the people who once controlled the islands. It is unfortunate that detailed accounts – personal narratives – of people who were held in bondage, such as the Chinese, Africans or East Indians of the Caribbean, are few and far between.

Illiteracy was widespread when the Caribbean Islands were under British control. This was because poor people, including those who were forced to settle the islands, were actively denied education. The paucity of personal narratives of poor people in written form makes it extremely difficult to access a range of differing perspectives and analysis of Caribbean history. Your story remains a mystery until you are successful in reconstructing your past. Our understanding of the people who helped to shape modern times will be lost forever unless families record their personal accounts. Collective family histories aggregate to the nation's history.

You can structure your narrative chronologically. Mention how individuals may have come by their names and how the names have been dispersed across the island and the world. Record your family's migration history from their continent of origin to their current settlement. Explain how your ancestors reached the shores of the Caribbean. Say something about the reasons for the migration, whether forcibly or otherwise. Retell the stories of the forebears who immigrated en masse to the British Isles – the Windrush generation. The Moving Here[22] website run by the National Archives documents working examples of how you might do this. Use maps to help you represent movements from one place to another.

You could start from the present working your way back in time and informing on what you discover along the way. References to documents and sharing your discoveries and disappointments would make interesting reading. Try not to let your scripts get out of hand by running on – think 'less is more'.

Alternatively, you could write individual profiles of direct ancestors, conveying the anecdotal stories and physical characteristics of individual family members (hair type, height, mannerisms). Include tales in order to bring your narrative to life. Conflicts with happy endings are interesting. Be warned: it is prudent to avoid stories with unhappy endings unless you're skilled in treating the information with due care and utmost sensitivity. Take care not to cause any offence by what you write. If in any doubt about the truth, use statements such as, 'it is said that' and place the story in quotes. Anecdotes about your ancestors' community would also be of interest. Draw on the accounts and experiences of individuals with similar backgrounds or employment. Explain things that happened in terms of what, when, how and why. Include simple family trees, maps and photographs.

When you have completed the narrative, consider publishing

it on the Internet. You could create your own site; it is easier than you think. Contact your Internet provider for information on how to do this. Whatever happens, write the narrative first and worry about the technicalities of publishing later. Personal webpages are now very common, and they make information more accessible to family members also.[23]

Part II

HISTORY UNMASKING
THE MYSTERY

The People of the Caribbean

Helping You to Trace Back

The search for who you are is more than a paper chase back in time. It is about valuing your cultural heritage. When you enter the world of genealogy, you become committed to reviewing and, if necessary, rewriting your history, as new and important facts emerge.

The search for identity begins with an understanding of the chain of events explaining how you find yourself occupying this space and time. Understanding migration histories helps to illuminate many a dark alley on the way to discovery. For example, 1838 was a significant date in Caribbean migration history. It marked the year slaves were freed. The ex-slaves travelled to other parts of the islands to settle and made a point of forgetting their traumatic past. The decades that followed would see proprietors migrate to other parts of the world. Property owners had as much as given up on some islands, heading for places as far away as Australia. You may find that your trail comes to an unexpected and sudden halt. Developing an appreciation of the key dates in Caribbean history can help you overcome some of these difficulties.

The section that follows describes the settlement of the Caribbean. African migration will be given more attention considering the extent to which the large majority of the population of the region can claim African ancestry.

The Amerindian people

Estimates of the original Amerindian inhabitants of the West Indies vary between 300,000 and several million. The Ciboneys are believed to be the first to have reached the Caribbean followed by the Arawaks and later the Caribs. Arawaks Taino (friendly people) and the Ciboneys occupied the northern larger islands of the Greater Antilles, the Bahamas and the Leeward Islands. The Caribs (who had a strong history of resistance to invasion) occupied the Guianas – today Guyana, Suriname and Cayenne.

The arrival of Columbus in 1492 in the 'West Indies' heralded demographic changes that had massive historical impact. Almost forgotten in the reminiscing about Colombus's arrival is the fact that within twenty years, the native Amerindian population of Hispaniola is estimated to have dropped from somewhere between 400,000 and 1 million to 30,000. This pattern was repeated all over the Caribbean where Europeans settled.

The European presence

It is often said that it was the environmental conditions of the Caribbean that actively conspired against large-scale European immigration. The evidence however suggests that when the Indian population was almost extinct, the capitalists of Britain sent for their own – the poor whites of Britain – to labour in their colonies. White people fared well performing heavy work near the Gulf of Mexico: they were sharecroppers in the southern USA; they were involved in the intensive cultivation of tobacco in Cuba; they were fishermen and agriculturists on the islands in the Dutch West Indies. White people had no problems adjusting to a life of hard work in the climate of Australia where an all-white policy existed, meaning that there was no non-white immigration.

Poor Britons were bound to serve for a fixed period and then to return home. They were convicts, many of them. Poor people who stole cloth, maimed or killed cattle or prevented customs officers in the execution of their duty were transported to the West Indies. In 1745, transportation was the penalty for stealing a silver spoon and a gold watch. Vagrants were also transported. Tens of thousands sailed from Bristol. Kidnapping was all too frequent in towns such as London and Bristol: 'Adults would be plied with liquor, children enticed with sweetmeats. The kidnappers were called 'spirits', defined as one that taketh upp men and women and children and sells them on a shipp to be conveyed beyond the sea.'[24]

When Diego Velasquez and his 300 men landed in Cuba for conquest, a hail of arrows greeted them. They came looking for gold, but they found agriculture, which was far more lucrative in the longer term. The indigenous Indians disappeared soon after.

The first Spanish royal permit for negro slaves was issued in 1513; by 1550 the movement of Africans was well established. Slavery did not end in Cuba until 1886.

The British and French carried out armed raids on Spanish possessions in the Caribbean from 1536 to the early part of the seventeenth century. The European presence resulted in the almost complete depopulation of the West Indies of its native Amerindians. Between 1630 and 1640 the Dutch colonised Aruba, Bonaire, Curaçao, Saint Eustatius, Saint Martin and Saba; the British controlled Antigua, Barbados and Nevis, and the French Martinique and Guadeloupe. Between 1697 and 1814 Britain and France engaged in conflict over the Caribbean Islands. In 1654, the chief British colonies were Suriname, Barbados, Jamaica, and the Leeward Islands.

The English
According to Eric Williams:

'The emigrants were packed like herrings... each servant was allowed about two feet in width and six feet in length in bed. The boats were small, the voyage long, the food, in the absence of refrigeration, bad, disease inevitable... seventy-two servants have been locked up below deck during the whole voyage of five and a half weeks, "amongst horses", that their souls, through heat and steamed under the tropic, fainted in them. "...it is hardly possible, to believe that human nature could be so depraved, as to treat fellow creatures in such a manner for so little gain".[25]

No, this was not, at the time, a description of the African experience of travelling through the Middle Passage; it was a description of white people transported to the Caribbean Islands to serve as indentured servants.

The English[26] settlers were recruited from England and from neighbouring islands such as Barbados and Nevis, and Suriname. Many died from disease. They were mainly farmers, men given small plots of land by the British. They remained loyal to the motherland, enjoying the same rights and privileges as they would have had at home in England.

The Industrial Revolution in Britain had massive consequences for the economy of the Caribbean Islands. The demand for sugar grew exponentially during the middle to late 1700s. Sugar production and other types of agriculture in the Caribbean started with small holdings, small farmers with their small workforce. As sugar took off, the small landholders were squeezed out by wealthy entrepreneurs who were quick to merge small holdings. The large plantations required a large workforce. As they spread rapidly across the Caribbean in a short period of time, it soon became obvious that sufficient numbers could not be supplied from Britain at the right place and at the right time. So it was to Africa they would turn, as the nearest source of abundant cheap labour.

Planters, merchants and the Anglican Church exerted influence over the government of the Caribbean Islands. They were all of European ancestry and in the main held an undying regard for their ancestral homelands outside the Caribbean. They ensured that Caribbean society emulated the mother countries. Even towards the end of slavery and beyond, descendents of Europeans held a remarkable loyalty to the ex-colonial masters. Caribbean-based newspapers were the means by which British settlers were kept informed of all that was happening in Britain and Europe.

By 1775, thirty per cent of the island's landholdings were held by absentee English owners, persons who resided in England and managed their plantations through Jamaican-based (often Irish and/or Scottish) overseers. West Indian planters were drawn back to the motherland like moths to the flame. They would send their children to be educated there if they didn't send them to the American mainland. Men with little or nothing in their pockets would journey to the Caribbean Islands to seek their fortunes. Their children or their grandchildren would in time return to the mother country with riches in abundance, and they would acquire estates and property. Families like the Beckfords, an old Gloucestershire family dating back to the twelfth century, who became one of the wealthiest sugar-producing families in the Caribbean, returned to build Fonthill mansion in the west of England. The Hibberts were West Indian planters, merchants and suppliers of cotton and linen checks to companies trading in Africa. There were also the Warners, a family which settled in the Leeward Islands, some in Antigua, Dominica, St Vincent and Trinidad. Joseph Warner became a surgeon at Guy's Hospital and was one of the leading practitioners of his day. West Indian planters sent their sons to public schools: Eton, Westminster, Harrow and Winchester. The great Charles James Fox, the prominent abolitionist, married a West Indian heiress with a fortune of £80,000.

Absenteeism had serious consequences for the islands, with a significant reduction in well-educated Europeans. Overseers and attorneys were left to manage (or mismanage) plantations. The reducing white population made it difficult to find people capable of participating in government of the islands. One individual might hold many offices.

At the time of emancipation in the 1830s, the number of absentee owners had risen to eighty per cent.[27] Yet, despite their lack of presence in numbers, the English influence was still strong.

Jewish people in the Caribbean

The history of Jewish people in Europe is full of attempts to restrict their potential to become the dominant force in the system of capitalism. Jewish diasporians were expelled from Spain in 1492 and resettled throughout the world. The British too were no different in their attempts to restrict Jewish engagement in capitalism and slavery. For example, Jamaican Jews were limited by law to ownership of two slaves, unless they owned plantations, and few did.

The British claimed the territory of Suriname in the mid seventeenth century. However, British citizens preferred not to settle there and so the government decided instead to attract Jewish people fleeing persecution on mainland Europe. The British government offered British citizenship, recognition of the Sabbath, and ten acres of land to build a synagogue.

In 1655, following the English Conquest, Rabbi Ben Israel from Amsterdam visited Lord Protector Cromwell and requested permission for Jews to settle in England (which Cromwell welcomed in the hope that the Jews would bring capital and mercantile knowledge). This implied the same permission would apply to settlement of the English colonies, leading to another influx of Jewish settlers to Jamaica from places like Amsterdam. All Jewish settlers had to be naturalised as British citizens and as such, they were entitled to own property – a right denied to Jews in Medieval Europe.

When the colony passed to the Dutch in 1667, many Jews moved to Barbados to retain their British citizenship. A Jewish community remained on Barbados until 1831, when a hurricane destroyed all of the towns on the island.

The British also attracted Jews to their colony in Jamaica.

There were settlements at both Kingston and Spanish Town and small landholdings in other parts of the island. The experiences of Jewish communities in Jamaica followed a pattern similar to that in Barbados.

The Scottish

The Scottish settlement of the Caribbean began around 1626. The first great wave started in 1654, when Oliver Cromwell transported five hundred Scottish prisoners of war, felons or political undesirables, such as the Covenanters.[28] They were sold as bond (indentured) servants to the English.

During the 1660s the Glasgow-based organisation called the Company Trading to Virginia, the Caribbee Islands, Barbados, New England, St Kitts, Montserrat and Other Colonies in America, established economic links with the West Indies. By the latter part of the seventeenth century, Scottish merchants, planters, seafarers, and transportees were to be found throughout the English and Dutch colonies of the Caribbean. In total, it is believed that as many as 5,000 Scots settled temporarily or permanently in the Caribbean before the Act of Union in 1707.

The English Privy Council regularly received petitions from planters requesting Scottish indentured servants. The British obliged by sending a wave of Scots when the Jacobite rebellion from 1745–46 failed.[29] A steady stream of indentured servants sailed from Scottish and English ports to the West Indies.

To a larger extent than elsewhere, the colonies of the West Indies attracted Scots with skills or money to invest. Scotsmen figured prominently in the sugar cane, cotton, and tobacco-growing businesses, a phenomenon which promoted trade between the Indies and the mainland ports of Boston, New York, Philadelphia, Charleston and Savannah. In due course, families moved between these various locations, and links were established. The Scottish population of the West Indies also increased when many loyalists took refuge there following the American Revolution.

A group of Scots arrived in Jamaica during the seventeenth century, comprising a number of refugees from the failed colony at Darien. By 1750 the Scots accounted for one third of Jamaica's white population.

Colonisation of Barbados began in February 1626–27 with the arrival of the *William and Mary*, containing eighty settlers and ten Africans.[30] By the 1650s the island was settled by the English, French, Dutch, Scots, Irish, Spaniards, Africans and what little there was left of the Amerindian population. Rioting and rebellion in England saw the transportation of waves of Scots and other Britons occupying the lowest echelons of society to the Caribbean.

In the compilation of *Scots in the West Indies, 1707–1857*, author David Dobson claims to have found the first listings of Scottish inhabitants of the West Indies. The entries are arranged alphabetically by surname and are sourced from Scottish newspapers such as the *Aberdeen Journal*, in which notices would appear seeking to employ managers and servants. In all, nearly 3,000 Scotsmen are identified, each by full name, island inhabited, date and source of the information, and sometimes by occupation, parents' names and education.

Scots were encouraged to go to Jamaica in the nineteenth century following emancipation. As part of its efforts to increase the white population of the islands in the British colonies, the government attempted to establish European townships. The practice started in 1834 when sixty-four Germans arrived from Bremen and settled near Buff Bay in a district that became known as Bremen Valley. It failed miserably and some moved to Clarendon to join the police. Next came 506 Germans, again from Bremen. In 1834 they settled on properties in St Ann's Bay, Montego Bay, Manchester, St Elizabeth and Clarendon. In 1835 a third wave of Germans arrived from Bremen.

Planters also recruited Europeans from England, Scotland and Ireland. The idea was to eventually create townships for the European immigrants in the island's highlands where the temperature was cooler. Many did not stay on these agricultural settlements and moved to the main towns instead.

The Irish

Political and religious nonconformists were transported to the sugar islands. This was the fate of the Irish. Between 1652 and 1659 over 50,000 Irish men, women and children were transported to Barbados and Virginia.[31] The author Sean O'Callaghan searched the library of the Barbados Museum and Historical Society and its files on Irish slaves. He documents the history of these people, their transportation, the conditions in which they lived on plantations as slaves or servants. One of the last shipments was made in 1841 from Limerick aboard the *Robert Kerr*.[32]

According to James F. Cavanaugh, Clann Chief Herald: 'If Queen Elizabeth I had lived in the twentieth century, she would have been viewed with the same horror as Hitler and Stalin.'[33] He was referring to the policy he claims was Irish genocide. He says that Elizabeth was only setting the stage for Oliver Cromwell to perfect. Cavanaugh's is the untold story of the Irish transportation to the Caribbean. It provides an interesting perspective of Europeans as slaves in the Caribbean. It is clearly an area that warrants more in-depth coverage.

He says that after the Battle of Kinsale at the beginning of the seventeenth century, the English were faced with a problem of some 30,000 military prisoners, which they solved by creating an official policy of banishment. Other Irish leaders had voluntarily exiled to the continent.

The Proclamation of 1625 decreed that Irish political prisoners be transported to English planters in the West Indies. However, from 1625 onward ordinary Irish people were sold as slaves to British planters in the West Indies. The punishment meted out to them is believed to have been no different to that endured by Africans. From 1629 Irish men and women were sent to Guiana,

Antigua and Montserrat. By 1637 a census showed that sixty-nine per cent of the total population of Montserrat were Irish slaves. But there were not enough political prisoners to supply the insatiable demand for labour, so every petty infraction carried a sentence of transporting. Slaver gangs combed the countryside to kidnap enough people to fill out their quotas.

In 1649, Cromwell landed in Ireland and attacked Drogheda, slaughtering some 30,000 Irish living in the city. Cromwell, it is said, reported: 'I do not think thirty of their whole number escaped with their lives. Those that did are in safe custody in the Barbados.'[34] A few months later, in 1650, 25,000 Irish were sold to planters in St Kitts. During the 1650s decade of Cromwell's Reign of Terror, over 100,000 Irish children, generally aged ten to fourteen years old, were taken from Catholic parents and sold as slaves in the Caribbean countries and other parts of the Americas.

Irish slaves revolted in Barbados in 1649. Rebels were hung, drawn and quartered and their heads were put on pikes, prominently displayed around Bridgetown as a warning to others.

In 1652, 12,000 Irish prisoners who failed to remove themselves from land and relocate to Shannon were transported to Barbados. It followed that 52,000 Irish, mostly women and sturdy boys and girls, were sold to Barbados and Virginia. Later, a further 30,000 Irish men and women were transported and sold as slaves.

A letter from Colonel William Brayne to the English authorities in 1656 urged the importation of Africans because 'as the planters would have to pay much more for them, they would have an interest in preserving their lives, which was wanting in the case of (Irish)...' Brayne charged that many Irishmen were killed by overwork and cruel treatment. The perception was that Africans were more durable in the hot climate, and caused fewer problems. The biggest bonus with the Africans though, was they were *not* Catholic, and any heathen pagan was, he believed, better than an Irish Papist. Irish prisoners were commonly sentenced to a term of service, so theoretically they would eventually be free. In practice, many of the slavers sold the Irish on the same terms as prisoners, for servitude of seven to ten years.[35]

In 1656, Cromwell's Council of State ordered that 1,000 Irish girls and 1,000 Irish boys be rounded up and taken to Jamaica to be sold as slaves to English planters.

After reviewing the profitability of the slave trade, Charles II chartered the Company of Royal Adventurers in 1662, which later became the Royal African Company. The Royal Family, including Charles II, the Queen Dowager and the Duke of York, then contracted to supply at least 3,000 slaves annually to their chartered company. They far exceeded their quotas.

So it was that the British government was concerned with satisfying planters' requirements for labour and increasing the white population in the colonies during slavery. But post-emancipation, a price was set on the head of Europeans immigrants, which involved the institution of ships like the *Robert Kerr*, known as 'man-traps', and sub-agents who wandered into quiet Irish towns with the sole aim of attracting people with the promise of free passage, high wages and the hope of bettering their lives.

According to James F. Cavanaugh, 'indentures bind two or more parties in mutual obligations. Servant indentures were agreements between an individual and a shipper in which the individual agreed to sell his services for a period of time in exchange for passage, and during his service he would receive proper housing, food, clothing, and usually a piece of land at the end of the term of service. Some of the Irish that went to the Amazon settlement after the Battle of Kinsale and up to 1612 are believed to have been exiled military who went voluntarily, probably as indentureds to Spanish or Portuguese shippers'.[36]

The planters quickly began 'breeding' the comely Irish women, not just because they were attractive, but because it was profitable, as well as pleasurable. Children of slaves were themselves slaves. Although an Irish woman may become free, her children could not. Naturally, most Irish mothers remained with their children after earning their freedom.

Planters then began to breed Irish women with African men to produce more slaves who had lighter skin and brought a higher price. The practice became so widespread that in 1681 legislation was passed 'forbidding the practice of mating Irish slave women with African slave men for the purpose of producing slaves for sale'.

This legislation was not the result of any moral or racial consideration; rather the practice was interfering with the profits of Britain's Royal African Company which had a monopoly on the triangular trade. A monopoly that the great British economist Adam Smith said had to go if Britain was to realise its economic growth potential. It is believed that Smith's arguments were a factor in winning converts to the abolition cause which won favour in 1807.

From 1680 to 1688, the Royal African Company sent 249 shiploads of slaves to the Indies and American colonies, with a cargo of 60,000 Irish and Africans. More than 14,000 died during passage. England shipped tens of thousands of Irish prisoners after the 1798 Irish Rebellion to be sold as slaves in the colonies and Australia.

Let the *Gleaner* have the last word on the effect of the contribution of the Irish to Jamaican culture: 'Yet, the Irish connection in Jamaica goes beyond the names of people, places and companies. It is found in a shared history of colonial domination and the achievement of independence in the same century. Yet, perhaps it is most strongly found in Jamaicans' love of laughter, horse racing, spirits, women and song.'[37]

The Chinese
Up to 2.5 million migrants from South and East Asia travelled to the Americas, mostly to the frontiers of western North America or the plantations of the Caribbean, Peru, and Brazil. Half of

this migration took place before 1885, after which the decline of indentured labour recruitment and the rise of anti-Asian immigration laws began to take effect. The Chinese were brought to the Americas from the 1840s to 1874: they came as indentured servants to Chile, Peru, Ecuador, Panama, Mexico and Cuba, in addition to the US.

Others also were sent to the Anglo-Caribbean under similar conditions. Human beings constituted the single largest 'export item' out of southern China through the British crown colony.

The Chinese immigrated to Trinidad as early as 1806[38] while significant Chinese emigration to Trinidad occurred mainly after emancipation. Compared to Indian immigration, the numbers were small, but the terms of indentured labour were the same. Indentured immigration ended in 1866, when the Chinese government required a return passage as part of the package.

After 1866, Chinese immigrants continued to trickle in, both from mainland China, and British Guiana, which had received a much larger share of the indentured Chinese. The Chinese labourers, like their Portuguese counterparts, left the plantations at the earliest opportunity to become shopkeepers, gardeners, and butchers. Their establishments were located primarily in rural villages, catering to the working classes. A further wave of immigration occurred after the Chinese Revolution in 1911, and remained high through the 1940s.

The Chinese immigrants came largely from the Hakka and the Punti communities in the Guangdong province. These immigrants, for the most part, abandoned their language and religions, and any sort of Chinese culture is now almost non-existent in Trinidad. Some prominent Chinese families include Achong, Aleong, Chin, Fung, Hochoy, Lai Fook, Lee, Lee Hueng, Lee Lum, Scott, and Wong.

The 1806 settlement in Trinidad left a mere handful of Chinese settlers on the island, most having returned to the East within a decade after arrival. The years 1852–54 saw the first attempts at an organised emigration effort from the Chinese mainland to the British West Indian plantations. In these years, seven vessels arrived in the West Indies (British Guiana, Trinidad and Jamaica) from both Fujian (Fukien) and Guangdong (Kwangtung) provinces. A further two vessels arrived in Jamaica with Chinese who had earlier gone to Panama. In all, they amounted to just over 2,000.

In 1853 the Dutch government in Suriname also began an experiment with Chinese labour, with one vessel bringing a small group of fourteen from Java. The years 1859–1866 were the high point of Chinese emigration to the British West Indies. The 1858–59 season was handled by a West India Committee appointee. The establishment of agencies at Hong Kong and Canton, and co-operation from China-based European missionaries and the Guangdong provincial authorities brought a certain measure of stability to the British emigration effort.

During these years, thirty-four vessels sailed for British Guiana, five for Trinidad, and one for British Honduras, with just over 14,000 Chinese. The Dutch government in Suriname also experimented with Chinese immigration during these years. Two further shipments from Macao had been attempted in 1858, under state auspices. With the end of slavery in 1863, the issue was again raised, and between 1865 and 1869 the private company, the Suriname Immigration Corporation, brought seven further vessels of Chinese from Hong Kong. In 1869, the Hong Kong government banned further shipments of contract labourers to non-British territories. All in all, about 2,530 Chinese arrived in Suriname between 1853 and 1869. The French West Indies also toyed with proposals for importing Chinese labour from Canton, and also from Shanghai. However, only a small number of vessels ever went to this part of the Caribbean, bringing just fewer than 1,000 to Martinique, Guadeloupe and French Guiana.

In 1874 and 1884, single sailings (to British Guiana and Jamaica) took place under a compromise contractual arrangement eventually worked out between the parties, and in 1879 and 1882, two vessels of free voluntary migrants made it (to British Guiana and Antigua) without contracts, but the peak of Chinese emigration to the British West Indies had already passed. Meanwhile, Suriname imported a further 115 Chinese from Java in several small shipments between 1872 and 1874.

The transition from indentured labour to free citizen for the Chinese had been similar to another minority immigrant group, the Portuguese (Madeirans). In the first place, the option of a free return passage to China did not exist, as it did with the Indians (only one third of whom ever exercised that option anyway). Those who did choose to return after their indenture period was over (or after a short sojourn within the society as free citizens) had to do so on their own. A significant number did, in fact. Most, however, remained in the Caribbean region, opting for a life outside of plantation wage labour. Many re-migrated or relocated within the Caribbean region itself, for example, Guianese to Trinidad, Suriname, Cayenne or Colon (Panama). In the fifteen-year period between 1872 and 1887 alone, about 3,000 re-migrated out of British Guiana for various destinations, mainly within the Caribbean. Many opted briefly for life as independent small farmers, before making other transitions. One experiment in British Guiana begun in the 1860s, the Hopetown Settlement, was the largest collective effort in this direction. Most became small traders, urban and rural, side by side with their other ethnic competitors (immigrants and natives). By the 1880s and 1890s the Chinese had moved out of agricultural life completely, and taken up their new roles as economic trader middlemen within the class/colour hierarchy of West Indian plantation society.

A decade later in the 1860s another set of Chinese arrived from Trinidad and British Guiana. There they had worked as indentured labourers in the cane fields until hurricanes and insects threatened their job security. Some 200 Chinese workers answered a call for three-year contract labourers in Jamaica to tend to the American-led large-scale planting of coconuts, bananas and sugar. When their three-year contracts were up, some continued in the fields even though they were not welcomed with open arms by the newly emancipated slaves who saw them as competition.

From the last two decades of the nineteenth century, and especially between 1910 and 1940, years that coincided with the domestic social turmoil in post-imperial China, another contingent of Chinese migrants made their way to the West Indies (and elsewhere in Latin America). These came as free migrants, usually on the basis of some family or district connection within the islands, and they gravitated right into the petty trading community, bypassing the earlier agricultural option of their predecessors. A simultaneous migration of Chinese to Cuban plantations during this period was quite specific to developments in that island, unlike the earlier period, which saw British Guiana as the major, and Jamaica as the least important, recipient of newcomers from China. This contrasted with the new migration, between 1918 and 1950, when up to 6,000 Chinese migrated mainly to Jamaica, then Trinidad and thirdly to British Guiana.[39] These migrants and their descendants formed the basis of the modern Chinese communities of the West Indies.

The Lebanese[40]

The Lebanese arrived in Jamaica towards the end of the 1800s. They were fleeing religious persecution at the hands of the Muslims, and attacks in the Middle East.

According to the Jamaica *Gleaner*: 'At the time, that region of the Middle East contained people from an area known as Mount Lebanon which was then part of Syria, hence the common confusion between the terms Syrian and Lebanese and why they tend to be used interchangeably.'

As with new immigrants before them, the Lebanese sought employment in agriculture.

The East Indians

From 1845 to 1921, over 36,000 East Indians, mainly of the Hindu faith, were brought to Jamaica. Close to two thirds of them remained. Following the abolition of slavery in the 1830s, after failed attempts to source much-needed labour through bountied European immigration, the Jamaican government turned to India and China. Indian labourers, who had already proved successful in Mauritius, were therefore considered to be a good bet for survival in Jamaica.

They were, however, paid less than the ex-slaves and therefore originally lodged at the bottom of society. Ironically, under the terms of their caste system, which valued light skin over dark, they in turn looked down on the ex-slaves. Relations between the two groups did not therefore begin on the best of footings.

The Indian government took great interest in indentured labour. Recruiting depots were established in Calcutta and Madras and agents were paid significantly less, per recruit, than for a European labourer. The government monitored recruitment, the terms and conditions of indentureship, and the guidelines for transport to Jamaica as well as eventual repatriation to India. Most Indians who signed on to indentureship did so with the hope of returning to their homelands with greater wealth and therefore better social positions. The government even appointed a Protector of Immigrants in the country of indenture.

Unfortunately, as the Protector was never an Indian national, he tended to be more interested in the welfare of the employers than the labourers; a sign that the programme would equal one of hardship for the labourers.

In order to sign on to an indentureship Indians were to appear before a magistrate, hold a government permit and fully understand the conditions of the labour contract. However, the contract was often explained in English and thousands of labourers simply put their thumb marks on the required line, without any true understanding of what awaited them following their journey across the sea.

African People

Introduction

Changes in the course of history always seem to be characterised by violence, the extremes of which know no boundaries circumscribed by skin colour. The moral outcry against slavery was stifled as the Spanish, the French, the British and other European countries fought each other to gain the upper hand.

Africans understand what it means for the grass, when two elephants fight. The history of Africans 'at home and abroad' is entwined with the stories of the super powers of 200 years past and their preoccupation with economic domination. Slavery had existed long before European contact with Africa, up to the beginnings of the Atlantic trade in the fifteenth century and through to the present day.

The events describing how it was that Africans came to settle the Americas is one of history's tragic if not shameful tales. It is remembered for the sheer scale of human suffering over a protracted period. Estimates of the numbers who fell victim are many times the millions who landed alive outside of Africa.[41]

The revolution in the French colony of St Domingo, when the African population overthrew the French colonisers to create the slave republic of Haiti, was the trigger for the British government's involvement in ending the slave trade. This was something that was never repeated in any other slave society. The wealth accumulated by West Indian planters supported the growth of cotton, iron, insurance, wool, sugar refineries and a range of capitalist ventures in Britain.

North America, which accumulated its wealth by growing the food to feed the slaves to ensure they produced more sugar for the mother country, needed to spend the money it had accumulated. This was beneficial to Britain's economy.

The fact that Africans in the Caribbean played a vital role in the development of North America and Britain is not in doubt. Indeed they played their part in shaping world history not just through their labour, but through their resistance to slavery. These actions helped to sweep away the economic advantages of the plantation system in the British West Indies. Africans in the Caribbean precipitated further the demise of an already declining industry by agitating for change.

African History Doesn't Begin with Slavery

First civilisation is estimated to date back 7,000 years, to the Nubian Kingdom of Ta-Seti in the north-east region of the continent. This was a dynasty of twelve pharaohs which ruled for 300 years. It had a superstructure and an infrastructure worthy of comment: government, culture, heritage, religion, cities, towns, ports and architecture. Then came the age of the pharaohs and their famous technological achievements, the Sphinx and the pyramids.

Egypt's decline was in free fall by the time of the twenty-fifth dynasty or 750 BC. When the Assyrians came in 663 BC, black dominance in world history was ended. The Persians, followed by the Greeks entered Egypt and knowledge of maths and astronomy found its way to Europe. And what of the blacks; some – the Kushites – stayed and flourished in the homelands for a while until 200 AD when the Romans invaded, as well as the Eritreans and Ethiopians.

The blacks who ruled Egypt fled the destruction of their

civilisations and enslavement as refugees, to form small communities in hill caves, and in isolated conditions they formed new languages. Fragmented remote communities began to distrust each other; the decline of culture was embedded. Distrust led to generations of feuding and tribalism, worsened by the slave trading in the north.

From this exodus of black Africans from the north-east and south-west came a golden age of civilisation in West Africa which dates back to about 300 AD. The ancient Hausa, Ghana, Mali and Songhai states and empires were known for their architecture, culture, government, trade, politics and religion. They covered vast areas, which were very different from the presently defined geographic areas; the result of colonial rule.

Africa was on a development continuum before European intervention from 1444 onward, when contact with the Portuguese heralded the dawn of the 'Atlantic Slave Trade' and dispersal of Africans to the Americas and northern Europe. It followed that the great achievements of Africans prior to the sixteenth century was systematically erased in order that capitalism could flourish.

When the Portuguese began their interaction with Africa, they could not have foreseen the extent of the destruction of millions of Africans over the centuries that followed.

Trafficking of Africans to the Caribbean

The trafficking of Africans began during the fifteenth century when the Portuguese laid claim to land near Gibraltar and soon encountered the African people. They saw themselves as devout Catholics taking 'heathens' as prisoners. By 1455 Portugal was importing close to 800 African slaves. It is believed that the Portuguese bartered for Africans peacefully instead of capturing them through warfare.

Sugar cultivation began in the Azores Islands, and as the demand for sugar grew, so did the demand for slaves to work the cane fields. By the sixteenth century, other countries started to compete in the sugar trade taking the trafficking of Africans to a new level.

Although the initial slave traders were Portuguese and Dutch, between 1750 and 1807, Britain 'dominated the buying and selling of slaves to the Americas'.[42] Shipbuilding flourished and manufacturing expanded: the 'process of industrialisation in England from the second quarter of the eighteenth century was to an important extent a response to colonial demands for rails, axes, buckets, coaches, clocks, saddles... and a thousand other things'.[43]

During the early 1500s, King Ferdinand of Spain gave authority for fifty slaves to go to the Spanish islands to work the mines. He ordered that they be the best and strongest available. From then on, only a few black Africans were sent each year to the Americas. Perhaps fifty annually, and not all at the same time, usually in trickles.

In 1505, Spain permitted seventeen blacks to be sent to Spanish islands in the Caribbean. Black Africans were considered accustomed to domestic animals and able to resist disease well. The Mandingo, Fula and Wolof peoples had an equestrian tradition whereas the indigenous Indians did not.

In Cuba, the first 300 Africans imported in 1524 started a migration that would see a black culture develop. It would be more profound than anywhere else in the Spanish empire.

In Puerto Rico, the first sugar mill was built in 1523. Seven years later the island's African population increased to nearly 3,000 slaves with only one in ten of the total population being indigenous European.

It is assumed that between 1500 and 1800 some 11 million Africans landed in the Americas as a result of the African slave trade. This is a conservative estimate narrowly based on surviving records. Approximately 10 to 11 million were recorded as having survived the Middle Passage – the journey across the Atlantic Ocean. There were many more who would have survived the 'illegal' trafficking which went unreported. It is estimated that

2 million Africans were transported to the British West Indies alone. They were captured by war, as retribution for crimes committed, or by abduction, and marched to the coast in 'coffles' with their necks yoked to each other. They were placed in dark dungeons at trading posts or forts to await the horrifying Middle Passage voyage between Africa and the Americas during which they were chained together, underfed, kept in the ship's hold; packed more like sardines than humans. Those who survived were fattened up and oiled to look healthy prior to being auctioned in public squares to the highest bidders. Jamaican slaves tended to come from the Ashanti, Mandingo, Ibo and Yoruba. Field slaves fetched between £25 and £75, while skilled slaves such as carpenters fetched prices as high as £300.[44] On reaching the plantation, they underwent a 'seasoning' process in which they were placed with an experienced slave who taught them the ways of the estate.[45]

In 1570, 2,000 to 3,000 Africans lived in Brazil. Between 1576 and 1591 it is estimated that between 40,000 and 50,000 African slaves, nearly all from the Congo, reached Brazil. The population of black slaves working on sugar mills in 1600 was about 15,000. The discrepancy between the import and the population draws attention to the brutality of the plantation system. Africans were expected to die after ten years. Plantation owners could be confident that any losses could be replaced quickly and cost-effectively from Angola or Congo.

By 1625 the total number of slaves taken out of Africa approached 200,000: 100,000 were transported to Brazil, 75,000 went to Spanish America, 12,500 to an island off the coast of Africa, and only a few hundred to Europe. These are the Africans that were known about.

By 1640, approximately 330,000 Africans had been transported to Spanish America, of which 150,000 were sent to Peru, 18,000 to New Spain and about 45,000 to Colombia. It is estimated that 16,000 were taken to the Spanish Antilles with 12,000 to modern

Venezuela. Africans were also transported to the silver mines of Bolivia.

By 1643, the Portuguese had sailed around southern Africa to Mozambique. They helped themselves to 4,000 to 5,000 Mozambiquans every year and transported them mostly to Brazil.

By 1650, 200,000 Africans were now being transported to the Americas. 100,000 probably went to Brazil and 50,000 to Spanish America. For the first time in the 1620s and 1630s, the English and French Caribbeans appeared as major customers. Nearly 20,000 Africans were transported to England and Barbados. 2,500 went to the French in Martinique and Guadeloupe. Many Africans would have arrived in the Caribbean on Dutch boats, including those taken to the Spanish empire. Angola was the main supplier during the said period. 170 Africans from Mozambique were transported to Barbados in 1682. By the end of the 1600s, the transport of Africans from European ports based along the coast of Africa had increased. It is thought that 370,000 were taken from 1650 to 1675, or little less than 15,000 per year.

The period 1675 to 1700 saw an estimated 600,000 transported, an average of 24,000 Africans per annum. The majority of these were sent to the islands of the Caribbean. The impact of this movement on Africa's decline as a comparatively developed continent is well documented in Walter Rodney's *How Europe Underdeveloped Africa*.

The status of the Portuguese as the largest shippers of slaves across the Atlantic peaked between 1721 and 1730. During this period they had shipped nearly 150,000 Africans – approximately 80,000 from Guinea and under 70,000 from Angola.

The British slave trade grew immeasurably in the early 1700s. In the ten years between 1721 and 1730 the British carried well over 100,000 Africans to the Americas. Nearly 40,000 went to Jamaica and over 20,000 to Barbados. Many were moved on to Cuba and elsewhere in the Spanish empire. About 10,000 went to South Carolina, and nearly 50,000 to the British Caribbean colonies.

During the 1770s, Britain carried less than 200,000 Africans because of the American War of Independence. France shipped a little less than 100,000 slaves during that period. In the decade that followed at least 750,000 Africans were shipped to the Americas. Britain accounted for as much as 325,000 with Liverpool the ever dominant city.

The white population of Jamaica declined between 1680 and 1700, falling from 9,000 to 7,000.[46] The African slave population grew from 10,000 to 45,000 between 1673 and 1703.[47] The end of the American War of Independence marked the beginning of the rush for African labour by Britain. From 1791 and 1802 France went to war with the slaves of St Domingo which was a major sugar-producing colony. This led to a shortage of sugar on the world market. Britain, in its determination to take advantage of the situation, raced to increase its sugar production and output. The result was fervent activity to dramatically increase the African population within the British colonies.

By 1793, the British slave trade was doing particularly well. And in Britain's prime colony of Jamaica, a record number of Africans were being imported – approximately 23,000 per annum. The total number of slaves imported between 1791 and 1795 was just under 80,000. The cultivation of sugar fuelled the thirst for more slave labour. And so it was that slaves would in no time at all vastly outnumber all other population groups. In 1791, Jamaica held 250,000 Africans in bondage. By 1797 the number was 300,000. The descendents of the slaves comprise the majority of the Caribbean's population.

British settlers in the Caribbean, feeling overwhelmingly out-numbered and facing an increasing culture of slave resistance, would absent themselves from their plantations. They headed for the United States where they had family and other property, or back to England to a more certain future.

British-produced sugar was under competitive threat from France whose sugar was much cheaper. The threats were reduced when Africans in the French colony of St Domingo (present day Haiti) decided to assert their right to be free. The war in St Domingo between 1791 and 1802, which CLR James wrote so vividly about in the *Black Jacobins*, was the chance for Britain to seize the opportunity to expand its sugar production which by default involved bolstering its position as the biggest importer of slaves into the sugar-producing colonies. Everything was as the British government wanted it until the war in St Domingo ended in 1802. By 1804, it dawned on the British that, as French interests returned to sugar, Britain would lose its competitive edge. Worse, Britain was the main supplier of the Africans France needed to fuel its upturn in fortune.

By 1807 legislation was passed to abolish the slave trade. The last day of Africans 'legally' landing in the British colonies was 1 March 1808.[48] Britain would concern herself chiefly thereafter with policing the waves, making sure that as few slaves as possible slipped illegally into the Americas and into the hands of its political and economic rivals.

The Maroons

When the English invaded Jamaica in 1655, the Africans who fought with the Spanish gained their freedom and then fled to the mountains. They became known as Maroons.[49] The term actually derives from the Spanish word *cimarron*, meaning wild or unruly. In the Caribbean the term became synonymous with runaway slaves. In Jamaica, Maroon settlements formed in the island's mountainous interior after the British invaded the island in 1655 and drove the Spanish out. Maroons retained strong African-derived traditions.

They were organised into a fighting force by Christoval Arnaldo de Ysasi before he too escaped to Cuba. By 1660, the Spanish had given up all attempts to recapture the island, but the Maroons continued to raid English plantations and settlements into the eighteenth century.

Jamaica's history recalls the Maroon Wars of 1729. Anxiety levels were high as the number of attacks on plantations by the Maroons of the interior grew. The plantocracy decided it would attempt to exterminate them, but the Maroons were able to overcome the island's militia using guerrilla tactics. The outcome was a treaty between the British militia and the Maroons led by Cudjoe. The treaty helped ensure that few plantation slaves escaped to the hills; those that succeeded were sure to be captured by the Maroons and either killed or returned to their masters. The treaty remained intact after the second Maroon War in 1795.

The word Maroon has almost become synonymous with Jamaica where slave revolts have been a salient feature of the island's history. It refers also to uprisings on other islands in the Caribbean.

The Koromantyn

Africans who came to the Caribbean from the Gold Coast were called Koromantyns. The term was used to identify Africans who displayed courage, robustness of attitude and physical strength. They were more likely to display unshackled designs to be independent and free.

Koromantyns caused great concern amongst a plantocracy living in constant fear of Africans and their descendents organising and striking for freedom. In fact, the term often referred to Akin, Fantin and Ashanti Africans. Maroons settlements were usually comprised of Koromantyns.

The Congoese

There are many references in advertisements placed in Caribbean local newspapers of the time to Congo slaves, and numerous slave traders dominated the Niger Delta, Cameroon and northern Congo. The Spanish Americans often referred to all Africans taken from this region as Congoese. Africans originating from the Congo as dominated by the Portuguese disembarked at Brazil.[50]

Plantation Society

It will not be enough to know that your ancestors were simply slaves – or masters of the property for that matter. You may begin to wonder about the actual physical environment. When you visit the Caribbean island, you might decide to track down the place where those feet walked in slavery times. It may mean very little until you understand more about plantation society. You may wish to know where on these properties your ancestors lived most of their life? Where would they have worked? What would the inter-action have been between Africans within the community and other cultures pre- and post-emancipation? You may wonder what they would have done day-to-day, from sun up until sun down.

Plantations were the places where the majority of Africans and their descendents lived and worked. The nature and quality of life on the plantations were very much determined by the decisions of planters and their supervisory representatives.

Of the islands within the British Caribbean, only Tobago, St Vincent and Antigua matched the concentration of slaves in very large plantations found in Jamaica.[51] Using Jamaica as a typical example of a sugar-producing island, you can gain a flavour of what life was like. You may even take your research further if you are researching one of the other islands.

A typical sugar plantation had a central location for the works – the manufacturing houses. There would be a plentiful supply of water through these works. It could be a well or pond if not a stream. The mills within the works complex would have been powered by cattle at least up until 1870. There would have been a slave village within close proximity to the works; the reason being that at certain times during the year, slaves were required to work through the night in the mills.

The works area would have included a mill, boarding house, curing house, and a steel and trash house. There would have been offices, a stock house, a hospital, a wheelwright, a carpenter and a blacksmith shop.

The master lived in a house on the hill – the 'Great House'. This enabled the master to survey all that he owned. The average distance between the village and works would have been about 400 yards. After emancipation, villages were located at a greater distance. There was a similar distance between the Great House and the works. The works covered approximately seven acres, the Great House three acres, and the villages eleven acres.

Land holdings would have averaged 300 acres. By the mid-1700s the average sugar plantation was 1,000 acres. A small percentage of proprietors would have owned more than 5,000 acres.

The cultivation of these lands took on greater proportions as plantations were abandoned when the island faced increasing competition from Brazilian and Cuban beet sugar. A loss in labour after emancipation in the 1830s and protective trade duties after the passing of the 1846 Sugar Equalisation Act in England contributed to a further demise.

In 1672 there were seventy plantations producing 772 tonnes of sugar per annum. During the early years of the eighteenth century the number of plantations in the British West Indies had risen at a phenomenal rate. This in turn increased the demand for more Africans in the Caribbean. There were six times as many slaves on Jamaican plantations as there were British. By 1712 Jamaica would not look back as it – for the first time – surpassed Barbados' sugar output. However, Great Britain became established as a major producer in 1730. 'During the 1770s there were over 680 much larger plantations, and by 1800, there were 21,000 English to 300,000 slaves, which increased to some 500,000 slaves by the eighteenth century. In 1820 there were 5,349 properties in Jamaica of which 1,189 contained over 100 slaves. The large estates had over 500 or 650 head of stock.'[52]

The British granted tariff protection on coffee in the 1790s. It was a time when French planters were fleeing to Jamaica from St Domingo. This resulted in an expansion of coffee production which peaked in 1814.[53] The price of coffee remained stable until 1870. After emancipation, Africans that took to the hills were likely to have engaged in coffee production; this required small landholdings as opposed to sugar which required large landholdings.

If your ancestors lived on coffee plantations, then these were most likely to be located up in the hills. You would have to imagine a different layout to a sugar estate. Sugar was confined to the lowlands, and coffee to the mountains. It was very rare for the two crops to be produced on a single property.[54] In some regions of the Caribbean, such as Guyana, sugar and coffee plantations were intermixed on the uniform coastal plain and their layouts were very similar.

As with sugar plantations, the coffee plantations had works in village house complexes situated centrally. Water was also a feature. There would be access roads from the field to the settlements. The expertise of the St Domingo planters was crucial in determining the layout of plantations. There was always a certain level of symmetry in the layout.

The workforce on each plantation was divided into gangs determined by age and fitness. On average most estates had three main field gangs: the first was comprised of the strongest and most able men and women; the second was comprised of those no longer able to serve in the first; and the third, of older slaves and older children. Some estates had four gangs, depending on the number of children living on the estate. Children started working as young as three or four years old.[55]

The social structure of plantation society was very rigid, as illustrated by the pyramid overleaf.

The product of forced miscegenation by British planters on African women was offspring classified by the plantocracy as 'coloured' (a term used in the former British colonies to describe people of mixed European and African descent). The Caribbean islands not under British control tended to free more so-called coloured people than the British. Manumission records or

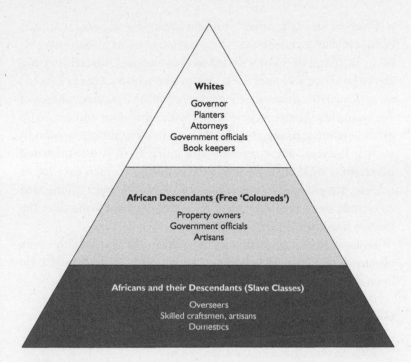

'freedom papers' are held at the National Archives in London. The records have been catalogued under Manumission's, but they are not well organised so it could take a degree of luck to find an individual even if you know who you are looking for. These records could appear in different forms: they may be part of the will or a separate document written by the master and given to the slave at the time of his freedom.[56]

The people classified as coloured may well have acquired their freedom through the manumission process. Masters at times also manumitted black slaves for various reasons, such as in reward for a lifetime of servitude. If, after gaining their freedom, they were to marry an African or a negro, then they would have lost their freedom. Any child, the offspring of any relationship between a coloured woman and an African, would have been born into slavery.

Free coloureds formed a middle group on the social ladder, between blacks and whites. The plantocracy was all too successful in instilling in them a desire to disassociate themselves from slaves but they were not accepted by the whites. Free coloureds were principally urban dwellers, participating in several phases of economic life. Some were provided with education and would go on to become artisans, merchants, mechanics, and professionals such as lawyers, schoolteachers and journalists. A few inherited plantations from their fathers. Free coloured women excelled as traders, shopkeepers, innkeepers and housekeepers. Many free coloureds were well educated, as education was valued as the vehicle for upward social mobility.

Despite their numbers and the education and wealth some obtained, free coloureds had no civil rights.[57] Many would have been slaves in everything but name.

Genetics

> And did those feet in ancient times
> Walk up on England's mountains green?

William Blake

Genetic genealogy has increased the possibilities for connecting with the ancient past. DNA testing is complicated because it can only be explained in scientific terms. A detailed scientific explanation is not within the scope of this book. There are companies that have compiled databases of thousands of people representing a number of ethnic groups from around the world. Each of these groups has genetic markers not found in any other ethnic group. The tests can confirm or deny connections to recent ancestors. This largely depends on the company and the extent of the database interrogated. The tests can answer whether two known individuals are related.

These companies claim to be able to trace at least one family bloodline to a specific geographical location on a given continent.

It is not the same as tracing your relations to a specific geographical location where they once lived. It is more accurate to say that they can trace the bloodline to a person who currently resides at a particular place today; one that shares the same umbilical bloodline as you. The reason for making the point is that genetic testing does not take into account the migrating nature of human beings over centuries.

Limitations

The landmark documentary *Motherland* showed some of the benefits and many of the pitfalls for anybody pursuing DNA testing. The documentary portrayed people with strong African features, being informed that their DNA profile indicated they were mainly white European. The crude, if not mischievous, interpretations placed on DNA results demonstrated how such testing can confuse if not undermine personal attempts to positively define one's identity. DNA results do not help you to define who you are, your experiences or the position you find yourself in today. This test will not provide you with a story you can pass to future generations.

DNA testing cannot replace paper research; it is not even a good substitute. Testing cannot provide you with specific information about a person in a given time at a given place. The DNA process may even generate more questions than answers. However, used in conjunction with other research techniques identified in this book, testing may help provide an emotional or spiritual connectivity with ancient ancestors that most people seeking an ancestral connection with Africa yearn for. This is where it's so powerful.

So how does it work?

There are two basic types of DNA tests available for genealogy: Y DNA Tests and mtDNA Tests. The Y DNA test is only available for males, since the test involves testing a small portion of the

Y chromosome, which is passed from father to son. Males have both an X and a Y chromosome. They receive the X chromosome from their mother, and the Y chromosome from their father. Females have two X chromosomes, one each from their father and mother.

'Both males and females inherit mtDNA from their mothers. Testing mtDNA provides information about the direct female line of the person, which would be their mother, their mother's mother, and so forth. MtDNA testing provides information about the original ethnic origin of your direct female ancestral line.'[58] It is also more likely to show European ancestry because of 'the dynamics of the plantation', as company president Gina Paige delicately puts it.

Genes are passed from generation to generation. Many pass unchanged, while others change considerably, as they are passed on. However, our close relatives will have similarities in the genetic information they hold. The closer the relative, the more similar the information in their DNA.

The results give the best estimate of a location for a maternal ancestor. It is a synthesis of all the geographical information from where a number of matches have been found. It is not precise; it is merely looking at where there are two or more locations and finding a centre point. For example you may have a match in India and seven in West Africa; the geographical centre is taken as a point in West Africa. People like to have a named town as a reference point, and companies will indicate this at the same time as conceding that there is no scientific basis for providing the name of the location as an ancestor's original town. This makes DNA testing interesting if not precise.

Samples are obtained from the inside of the cheek for the analysis. A blood sample is not necessary. You open the sterile envelope, swab the inside of the cheek, put it back into the envelope, seal it and mail it off.

The cost of the tests can be prohibitive. Any decision to

Case Study 17

Objective: To connect with the ancient African ancestors
DNA Result:
Name: Paul Crooks.
Nearest location: Am Raya, Chad
Best matches: Fulbe and the Kunari people

There are two people living in Chad who share the same mother line as me. Another person living in Saudi Arabia also shares the same mother line. It is not possible to say for sure whether I have an ancestor that originates from the location where the two best matches were found. They are people that have been sampled and are included in the database. Neither do I know for sure how far back in time I would have to go to find the maternal grandmother we all share. There has been much migration up, down and across Africa over the last 10,000 years.

West Africa was sparsely populated up until about 300 to 400 years ago. Chad was fairly remote from the European slave trade which took place from the West African coast 400 miles inland. So the evidence suggests that my maternal grandmother would probably go back a few generations before slave trade with Europe. Chad would have been more seriously affected by the Arab slave trade which existed centuries before and continued during the European slave trade. This may even explain the other match in present-day Saudi Arabia.

Another interpretation could be explained by the 'black flight' from Egypt when the Arabs and other people of the north made their presence felt. The descendents of the pharaohs fled east, and south-west towards the Gold Coast. The evidence suggests that some of the current rituals and practices of the people of Ghana appear to be Hebrew in origin and traceable back to the land of Egypt. My maternal grandmother could therefore have lived in that region within the last 400 to 1,000 years if she was part of the flight from Egypt. If black Africans had always lived in that region then it is possible that the maternal grandmother that I share with the other dots on the map could go back 10,000 years.

undertake DNA testing should be based on judgements about affordability. If you have surplus cash then all well and good. You may decide to use your tests to develop positive links with specific communities in Africa. Whatever you decide to do, nothing can replace the excitement of making a tangible connection through systematic research.

Over time, as the database grows larger, the results will become more and more precise.

It is impossible to know for sure what conclusion to draw from DNA testing. Despite the limitations, there is something uplifting about having a scientific link to the ancient ancestors than to have nothing at all.

The Islands of the Caribbean

The written history of the British Caribbean has been to a large extent based on records housed in national libraries and archives in Great Britain and the Caribbean Islands themselves. If you are going to use your time efficiently when searching British archives, understand that you'll be extremely challenged to find information about a specific island during periods when it was not under British control. Remember the British, French and Spanish were constantly vying for economic control of the islands. If you are searching for an ancestor who may have lived in St Lucia during the French colonisation, then be sure you are literate in French or know somebody who is and would be prepared to help you with research – possibly at the French public records.

This section is intended to provide a brief history of some of the main islands in the Caribbean. When setting objectives, be clear as to whether you wish to go down the line which takes you deep into French, Spanish, Portuguese or Dutch history.

Dominica[59] – The Igneri Indians, originally from South America, settled this island almost 2,000 years ago. They became extinct around 400 BC when Caribs populated the Caribbean. The English and French fought each other to colonise Dominica during the 1600s, over a hundred years after the failed attempt by the Spanish. The English and the French fought over Dominica as they did over much of the Caribbean. It wasn't until 1761 that the British wrested the island from the French. During the American War of Independence, when the British militia were preoccupied with the United States, France decided it would take advantage and attack the British in Dominica. They succeeded in 1778 but four years later, after the war, the British again wrested Dominica from France. The names of locations within the island are therefore a mixture of French, English and Carib. From 1785–86 it was the turn of the Africans enslaved on the island to attack the English. They were unsuccessful, but they tried again in 1815.

St Lucia[60] – The history of St Lucia bears similarities to Dominica, with the French and British vying for control of the island and it was the French who first settled the island. By 1780 it had twelve settlements and a number of large sugar plantations. The first settlement was at Soufrière in 1746. In 1782 the British invaded at the 'Battle of Cul de Sac'. By 1814, they managed to gain control of the island.

Grenada – The English in 1609 established Megrin Town. The Caribs wasted little time in driving them away as they did the French when they attempted to colonise the island in 1639. Determined, the French returned once more, and the Caribs eventually accepted their presence only as a possible deterrent to the English who had massacred Caribs in St Kitts. In 1675 the Dutch took control of the island briefly before the French returned and held on to it until 1763 when it was ceded to the British under the Treaty of Paris. The island changed hands again when in 1779 the French took control.

St Kitts (formerly St Christopher) – In 1493 Colombus named it after St Christopher, his patron saint. The period 1623–24 signalled the beginnings of European colonisation starting with the English who shortened the name to St Kitt's Island. St Kitts was held jointly by the English and French from 1628–1713. There were many Irish indentured servants in St Kitts. The Protestant English and Scots had great difficulty resolving issues with the Catholic Irish. During the seventeenth century, intermittent warfare between French and English settlers ravaged the island's economy. Governor Warner feared that in wartime the Irish might side with the Catholic French colonies on the ends of the island. He decided to deport many to the islands of Montserrat and Antigua. The Treaty of Utrecht ceded St Kitts to Great Britain in 1713. The French seized both St Kitts and Nevis in 1782. The Treaty of Paris in 1783 definitively awarded both islands to Britain.

Barbados – The English landed on the island in 1625, and by 1627 it was occupied. People with good financial backgrounds and social connections with England were allocated land. Within a few years much of the land had been deforested to make way for tobacco and cotton plantations, and then sugar cane. White civilians who wanted to emigrate overseas could do so by signing an agreement to serve as a planter in Barbados for a period of five or seven years. White people were also kidnapped, and convicted criminals were shipped to Barbados. Descendants of the white slaves and indentured labour (referred to as redlegs) still live in Barbados, amongst the black population in St Martin's River and other east coast regions. At one time they lived in caves in this region.

Barbados became the richest colony in English America as a result of Sephardic Jewish capital, Brazilian-Dutch expertise, and African labour.

Martinique & Guadeloupe – The Carib tribes were massacred by 1658. Any survivors fled to the islands of St Martin or Dominica, to live on a reserve. Despite their military defeat, some Caribs remained in Martinique, progressively mixing with more recent settlers. The labour force was composed of Europeans engaged in three-year contracts, and a few African slaves. With the arrival of Dutch sugar manufacturers from Portuguese-owned Brazil, a new economic era began. Martinique, as well as most of the Caribbean Islands, became a major sugar producer at the end of the 1600s.

Though originally called Karukéra (Island of Beautiful Waters) by the Carib Indians, the island was renamed after the famous sanctuary of Santa Maria de Guadalupe de Estremadura.

Europeans did not take a great interest in the island until the seventeenth century. For a brief period the Spanish had tried to settle Guadeloupe, but they were prevented by the ferocious Carib Indians. Then around 1635, the French began to colonise the island. Slavery was established by 1644. Britain occupied the island after many a battle with the French from 1759 to 1763. France took control in exchange for all French rights to Canada. Finally, it was designated as French through the 1815 Treaty of Paris.

What Do We Teach Our Young?

'If violence is constantly portrayed as normal on the television screen it will help to create a violent society.'

Mary Whitehouse, 5 May 1964

Today's struggle is for the minds of our young. The battle-ground is in the home, schools and higher places of learning. Family history could be a weapon of choice.

We should encourage our young to explore their cultural identity and that of their peers. This is the vehicle for engendering respect for themselves and others. Not only should they learn to appreciate where their parents, grandparents and great-grand-parents came from but they should learn to appreciate the same about their peers.

The systematic process of seasoning has had a long-lasting impact, starting a cycle that has been passed down to successive generations. Second and third generation African Caribbean people born in Britain are now being encouraged through the school system, to embrace the 'black presence' in Britain, going back to the Romans. To be benign, this represents a misinformed, even desperate, attempt to underpin the process of integration into British society. It has the potential to exacerbate the identity crisis manifest in the playgrounds of the Caribbean experience. The mere mention of slavery has, in the past, invoked unspoken remembrance of the pain and suffering of our black forebears. Increasingly educators, on the subject of slavery, have been instrumental in creating a new pride in our heritage. The educators having the greatest impact are the ones pointing to the many instances when our forebears maintained their dignity in the midst of an inhumane system. African Caribbean communities no longer have a reason to be ashamed that some of their forebears were Africans held in bondage. This is important because prosperous communities unashamedly embrace their culture and heritage even when they are displaced from their country of origin.

They instil in their young a sense of pride about who they are and where they came from. Prosperous communities place great emphasis in their teachings on the strength their ancestors deployed in overcoming past struggles. Individuals who have successfully researched their family histories also appreciate the importance of passing on information about their people who were once the history-makers of their time.

Young people who receive information about family history should be equipped to interpret and express their personal histories as individuals and in groups. They will recognise their potential to use the information to positively influence and shape the communities in which they live, as they mature to become adults. The potential for such positive outcomes should not be underestimated. It is important that young people understand the role of their forefathers on the stage of history. When Caribbean islanders (the Windrush generation) migrated to the British Isles after the Second World War, they could not have grasped the historical significance of what they had done. They were making history and they did not know it. The same will be said of Asians during the 1970s and more recent migrants and refugee communities fleeing unstable regimes in their homelands during the 1980s, 1990s and this new millennium.

Ultimately, it is the responsibility of parents – as teachers – to ensure that memorabilia, documentation and knowledge from the family archive is preserved then passed on using the effective methods and the technologies available. By encouraging young people to appreciate their participation on the stage of making history, they will understand how future generations will judge them by their acts or omissions here in the present.

You can begin by involving them in creating their family trees going back as far as their grandparents. Schoolteachers can do something similar at any time with children aged eight and upwards. Teachers can support young people to think about family history. This can be accomplished by tasking young people with completing the family tree template provided in the Resources section at the end of the book. When completed, encourage them to discuss it amongst their peers. Any gaps in the family tree can be talked about with parents as homework. By working in groups, young people can gain an appreciation of their peers' background.

It is important that parents teach their young about the family legacy. Teaching does not mean sitting them down in front of a makeshift blackboard and lecturing. Sensitivity to the way young people learn will bring its own rewards. The time has come to transform the way history is taught. It is very rare to meet a young person that understands the point of learning history and why, along with English, maths, science and geography, it has always been a core feature of any structured education programme.

Building Blocks of History

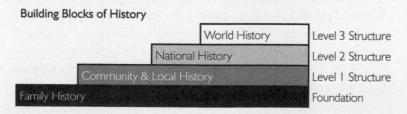

The above suggests a model for educators seeking to engage

young people's interest in the subject of history from an early age. It starts with a knowledge and awareness of self and family history as the building block on which discourse in history and social issues develop as young people mature.

Children aged five to seven

When engaging five- to seven-year-olds in family history, it is important to bear in mind that they learn best when they are active. They need frequent breaks from the tasks set. They like to do things that are fun for them and involve use of energy.

For parents, a simple interactive exercise would be appropriate. Children like to be told stories, particularly at bedtime. Try, every so often, to substitute the usual bedtime story format of reading a tale from a book, with the story told to you by your parents or your grandparents. Try picking something comical to begin with, perhaps an old family tale. If it was scary, then mix it with some of the traditional tales steeped in superstition to add entertainment value – provided your child likes to hear scary stories.

Teachers working with groups could ask children to create a family tree. Ask children first, to complete what they know about themselves. Ask them to include their name, date of birth and place of birth (hospital, town and country). Then ask the children to complete as much as they know about their parents. How many will know their parents' full names including middle names? How many will have any idea of where their parents were born? How many will know the ages of their parents and equate this to a date of birth? How many will be curious to find out information that they don't already know. The same questions should be posed in relation to the child's grandparents. Not all children will have the full set of information. Completing the gaps and information about their parents could be set as a piece of homework. The aim is encourage the child to interact with their parents on issues of family history. It may be the first chance they have to play with interview techniques. How good will they be at getting the information from their parents. The children should be asked to 'show and tell' one thing they found out about the person they live with (accepting that not all children will live with both parents or have birth grandparents).

Children aged eight to ten

Eight to ten-year-olds will be interested in people, aware of differences, willing to give more to others but expect more. They will be busy, active, full of enthusiasm, may try too hard. They will be sensitive to criticism, recognise failure, and have the capacity for self-evaluation. They will be capable of prolonged interest, able to hold conversations and sometimes be outspoken. They will be eager to answer questions and be very curious.

Teachers working with these groups could ask young people to complete the family tree template working together in small groups. Young people should spend time completing information about their parents, grandparents and if possible great-grandparents (this should be explained to them). They could also complete information about the person they live with which may not necessarily be any of the above. Young people should be encouraged to share information that they are comfortable sharing with each other. They should be encouraged to talk about where their parents originally came from. Follow up by asking them to think about what brought them to the place where they live today. When they have completed the names, dates and places and briefly interacted with each other, they should be asked to give feedback to the class regarding one thing they have learned about their classmates origins. Find out whether they can point to any places of origin on a map or atlas.

They should be encouraged to go home and complete the gaps in the information about their parents and grandparents and great-grandparents if that's possible. They should also be encouraged to write a couple of sentences about each generation using the template focusing specifically on something they didn't know before they interacted with their parents on the subject. It might be a short story, it might be physical or mental characteristics: anything that the child found interesting.

Young people aged eleven plus
The same exercise can be repeated for this group only with more in-depth discussion in groups. These young people should be asked to write more about their family histories, concentrating on the struggles that their parents or grandparents had to go through in order to establish their families. They should also be encouraged to write a few sentences about perceived family values or physical and mental characteristics. Teachers must be sensitive to the needs of some young people to want to withhold certain information. So the emphasis should always be on positive attributes of family. The emphasis should be on self-evaluation and self-discovery and identity. Young people should be asked a simple question: who are you? They should respond by saying: I am...

If these exercises are repeated at each of the key stages mentioned above then a seed will have been planted that may grow inside the young person and flourish. When curiosity about the origins of the family, values and main characteristics grows, then these young people may decide to embark on a journey of self-discovery. Maybe then they will become people empowered to be positive role models.

Notes

1. Cornel West. *Race Matters* (Beacon Press, 1993) p. 17
2. Ibid.
3. Ibid., p. 5
4. Ibid., p. 3
5. Ibid., p. 15
6. From *Indaba, My Children* by Credo Mutwa, first published in Great Britain by Canongate Books Ltd, 14 High Street, Edinburgh, EH1 1TE. First published in South Africa in 1964 by Blue Crane Books
7. http://www.bbc.co.uk/worldservice/africa/features/ storyofafrica/1chapter1.shtml
8. The National Archives, Kew: CO 137/144, pp. 157–162
9. *Jamaican Genealogy Sources for Those Beginning Their Search.* Available from: http://users.pullman.com/mitchelm/ beginscs.htm (accessed 30 July 2007)
10. http://catalogue.rgs.org/uhtbin/webcat
11. B.W. Higman. *Jamaica Surveyed Plantation Maps and Plans of the 18th and 19th Centuries* (Institute of Jamaica Publications Ltd, 1988)
12. Richard Hart. *Slaves Who Abolished Slavery: Blacks in Bondage* (University of the West Indies Press, 1980) p. 196
13. Ibid., p. 197

14. Richard Hart. *Slaves Who Abolished Slavery: Blacks in Rebellion* (University of the West Indies Press, 1980)
15. Richard Hart. *Slaves Who Abolished Slavery, Blacks in Rebellion* (University of West Indies Press, 2002) p. 336
16. Eric Williams. *Capitalism and Slavery* (André Deutsch Ltd, 1964) p. 92
17. Refer to Resources at the end of the book for contact information.
18. The British Library. *India Office Records: History and Scope* [online]. Available from: http://www.bl.uk/collections/iorgenrl.html (accessed on the 30 July 2007)
19. The British Library. *India Office Records: History and Scope* [online]. Available from: http://www.bl.uk/collections/oes/caribbean/images/deathlistcambodia.jpg
20. David Eltis, Queen's University; Stephen D. Behrendt, Victoria University of Wellington; David Richardson, University of Hull; Herbert S. Klein, Columbia University
21. For further information, refer to: Louis E. Wilson. *The Krobo People of Ghana to 1892, A Political and Social History* (Ohio University Press, 1991)
22. www.movinghere.org.uk
23. An extract from the Crooks of Jamaica site has been provided in the appendices of this book.
24. Eric Williams. *Capitalism and Slavery* (André Deutsch Ltd, 1964) p. 11
25. Eric Williams. *Capitalism and Slavery* (André Deutsch, 1964) pp. 13–14
26. Dr R. Tortello. 'Out Of Many Cultures The People Who Came, The English', *Jamaica Gleaner*. Available from: http://www.jamaica-gleaner.com/pages/history/story0063.html
27. See P. Sherlock; H. Bennett. *The Story of the Jamaican People* (Ian Randle Publishers, 1998) p. 159
28. http://www.newworldcelts.org/carribean.html

29. Dr. R. Tortello. 'Out Of Many Cultures The People Who Came, The Jews In Jamaica', *Jamaica Gleaner*. Available from: http://www.jamaica-gleaner.com/pages/history/story0054.htm

30. http://www.newworldcelts.org/carribean.html

31. Sean O'Callaghan. *To Hell or Barbados: The Ethnic Cleansing of Ireland* (Brandon, 2001)

32. *Jamaica Gleaner* (online)

33. J. F. Cavanaugh. 'New World Celts, Caribbean Celts, Irish Slaves' [online]. Available from: http://www.newworldcelts.org/irish_slaves.htm (accessed 30 July 2007)

34. https://www.indymedia.ie/article/78714

35. http://www.newworldcelts.org/irish_slaves.htm

36. http://www.raceandhistory.com/cgi-bin/forum/webbbs_config.pl/noframes/read/1638

37. Dr R. Tortello. 'Out Of Many Cultures The People Who Came, The Arrival Of The Irish', *Jamaica Gleaner*. Available from: http://www.jamaica-gleaner.com/pages/history/story0058.htm

38. TriniGenWeb. 'Asians. The Chinese'. Available from: http://www.rootsweb.com/~ttowgw/comings/chinese.htm

39. Walton Look Lai. *The Chinese in the West Indies, 1806–1995, a documented history* (University of West Indies, 1996)

40. Dr R. Tortello. 'Out Of Many Cultures The People Who Came, The Arrival Of The Lebanese'. Available from: http://www.jamaica-gleaner.com/pages/history/story0056.htm

41. Walter Rodney. *How Europe Underdeveloped Africa* (Bogle L'Overture Ltd, 1988) p. 96

42. *Jamaica Gleaner* (online); Also see P. Sherlock; H. Bennett. *The Story of the Jamaican People* (Ian Randle Publishers, 1998)

43. Ibid.

44. www.jamaica-gleaner.com/pages/history/story0059.htm

45. For further information refer to: Olive Senior. *The Encyclopaedia of Jamaican Heritage* (Twin Guinep Publishers, 2003)

46. J. Voorthuis. 'The Architecture of Exploitation', (online). Available from: http://www.voorthuis.net/Pages/SLAVERY.htm [accessed 30 July 2007]

47. B. W. Higman. *Jamaica Surveyed Plantation Maps And Plans Of The 18th And 19th Centuries* (Institute of Jamaica Publications Ltd, 1988) p. 8

48. Richard Hart. *Slaves Who Abolished Slavery: Blacks in Rebellion* (University of West Indies Press, 2002) p. 165

49. For further information refer to: Olive Senior. *The Encyclopaedia of Jamaican Heritage* (Twin Guinep Publishers, 2003) pp. 5; 446

50. See Hugh Thomas. *The Slave Trade, the History of the Atlantic Slave Trade 1440–1870* (Papermac, 1998) pp. 203; 220; 227

51. J. Voorthuis. http://www.voorthuis.net/Pages/SLAVERY.htm

52. Dr R. Tortello. 'Out Of Many Cultures The People Who Came'. Available from: http://www.jamaica-gleaner.com/pages/history/story0056.htm

53. B. W. Higman. *Jamaica Surveyed Plantation Maps and Plans of the 18th and 19th Centuries* (Institute of Jamaica Publications Ltd, 1988) p. 9

54. B. W. Higman. *Jamaica Surveyed Plantation Maps and Plans of the 18th and 19th Centuries* (Imstitute of Jamaica Publications Ltd, 1988) p. 159

55. For further information, refer to: Olive Senior. *The Encyclopaedia of Jamaican Heritage* (Twin Guinep Publishers, 2003) p. 207

56. C.L. Blockson. *Black Genealogy* (Baltimore: Black Classic Press, 1977) p. 80

57. V. Satchel. 'Jamaica.' Africana.com, 1999 (online). Available from: http://www.hartford-hwp.com/archives/43/130.html (accessed 30 July 2007)

58. Worldwide Ancestry Research Services [online]. Available from: http://www.wars-genealogy.co.uk/genetic_genealogy.cfm (accessed on 30 July 2007)

59. Sky Views. 'The History of Dominica' (online). Available from: http://www.skyviews.com/dominica/history.html (accessed 30 July 2007)

60. St Lucia Tourist Board. 'History of St Lucia' (online). Available from: http://www.geographia.com/st-lucia/lchis01.htm

Appendix 1

Parish Index of Baptisms 1800–1836

Index for the baptism records 1800–1836. Signposts to the full baptism record for John Alexander Crooks.

Appendix 2

Parish Index – Jamaica 1868

Index to the baptism record 1868. Signposts to the full record for Robert Crooks, the author's great-grandfather, and his parents.

Appendix 3

Parish Registration – Baptism Record, Jamaica, 1813

Baptism record, Cousins Cove Sugar Plantation, Hanover, Jamaica, 1813, includes the name John Alexander Crooks.

Appendix 4

Mass Baptisms 1814

A Return as copied from the Parish Register, and the Estate Books of Slaves baptised in the Parish of Hanover Jamaica, by the Revd Daniel Warner Rose Rector, in the Years 1814. 1815. 1816, and up to the 25th June 1817 with the Names of the Properties and Proprietors to whom they belong, and the time when they were baptised ——

160

Properties or Place of Baptism	Proprietors	Number Baptised	When Baptised
At Green Island	To various owners	22	February 5th 1814
Bounty Hall	D. Cameron Esqr	9	12
ditto ditto	Mr Ewar	4	12
ditto ditto	Various owners	17	12
Davis's Cove	Ro. Dickson Esqr	36	April 2
Argyle	John Malcolm Esqr	64	March 22
Burnt Ground	J. H. James Esqr	120	March 23
Cousin's Cove	Ro. Dickson Esqr	124	April 3
ditto	Mrs Brown	22	3
Grange	J. Stales Douglass Esqr	210	
Glasgow	Rt Wallace Esqr	177	30
ditto	Various owners		
Haughton Court	Sir S. Taylor	28	July 16

A list of baptisms by Reverend Daniel W. Rose in 1814. Includes baptisms of slaves on Cousins Cove and William Brown's plantation.

Appendix 5

Passenger List for the Ship *Irpinia*, 1957

The passenger list for the ship *Irpinia*, Southampton, 1957. It includes full name of George Crooks, first address in the UK and date of birth.

Appendix 6

Slave Register – Hanover, Jamaica, 1817

An extract from the Return of Slaves on the Cousins Cove Sugar Plantation, Hanover, Jamaica, 1817 including the name of John Alexander Crooks, the author's great-great-great-grandfather.

Appendix 7

Triennial Update 1823

The Return of Slaves on Cousins Cove in the Parish of Hanover, Jamaica, 1823. The second update to the 1817 register, which includes Sarah Brown, the author's great-great-great-grandmother and her firstborn, John.

Appendix 8

Slave Register Triennial Update – 1826

Slave register updated. An extract of the additions and deletions to the Cousins Cove Sugar Plantation, Hanover, Jamaica, 1826, including the recorded death of the author's great-great-great-great-grandmother documented here as Judy Brown.

Appendix 9

Compensation Claim, Cousins Cove, Hanover, Jamaica, 1834

A Compensation Claim by Neil McCullum for the release of 187 slaves from captivity, including William Crooks, the author's great-great-grandfather.

Appendix 10

A List of Inhabited Islands in the Carribean

The number of maps held by the Royal Geographical Society for each of the Caribbean Islands.

Anguilla (UK)	1
Antigua and Barbuda	
Antigua	76
Barbuda	33
Aruba (Netherlands)	2
Barbados	
Barbados	52
Culpepper Island	0
Pelican Island (now absorbed into Barbados)	1
Belize	158
Ambergris Cay	2
Caye Caulker	0
Glover's Reef	0
Hicks Cays	0
Lighthouse Reef	5
South Water Caye	0
Turneffe Islands	0
British Virgin Islands (U.K.)	21
Anegada	5
Beef Island	1

Bellamy Cay	0
Cooper Island	1
Frenchman's Cay	1
Great Camanoe	0
Guana Island	0
Jost Van Dyke	0
Little Thatch	0
Marina Cay	0
Mosquito Island	0
Nanny Cay	0
Necker Island	0
Norman Island	0
Peter Island	35
Prickly Pear Island	0
Saba Rock	0
Salt Cay	0
Tortola	0
Virgin Gorda	0
Cayman Islands (U.K.)	12
Cayman Brac	1
Grand Cayman	3
Little Cayman	1
Colombia	335
San Andrés and Providencia	1

Cuba

Cuba	155
Isla de la Juventud	1
Dominica	30

Grenada

Carriacou	2
Grenada	25
Petit Martinique	0
Guadeloupe (France)	13
Basse-Terre	1
La Désirade	0
Grande-Terre	0
Marie-Galante	0
Iles de la Petite-Terre	0
Saint-Barthélemy	0
Terre-de-Bas (Les Saintes)	0
Terre-de-Haut (Les Saintes)	0
Saint-Martin (same island as Sint Maarten)	21
Hispaniola (Haiti and the Dominican Republic)	22
Haiti	30
Dominican Republic	33
Honduras	168
Barbaretta (Islas de la Bahía Department)	0
Cayos Cochinos (Islas de la Bahía)	1
Guanaja (Islas de la Bahía)	0
Roatán (Islas de la Bahía)	0
Swan Islands	0
Útila (Islas de la Bahía)	0
Jamaica	285

Martinique (France)	5
Mexico	1227
Cancún	0
Isla Contoy	0
Isla Cozumel	0
Isla Mujeres	0
Montserrat (U.K.)	29
Netherlands Antilles (Netherlands)	9
Bonaire	1
Curaçao	12
Saba	9
Sint Eustatius	2
Sint Maarten (same island as Saint-Martin)	0
Nicaragua	81
Corn Islands	0
Cayos Miskitos	0
Panama	304
San Blas Islands	0
Bocas del Toro	0

Puerto Rico (UK)

Culebra	15
Mona	12
Puerto Rico	44
Vieques	1
Saint Kitts and Nevis	11
Nevis	26
Saint Kitts	11
Saint Lucia	15
Saint Vincent and the Grenadines	17
Bequia	1

Canouan	0	Parrot Cay	0
Mayreau	0	Pine Cay	0
Mustique	0	Providenciales	0
Palm Island	15	Salt Cay	0
Petit Saint Vincent	0	South Caicos	0
Saint Vincent	34	U.S. Virgin Islands (U.S.)	1
Union Island	2	Hassel Island	0
Young Island	9	Saint Croix	1
Trinidad and Tobago	64	Saint John	5
Tobago	98	Saint Thomas	2
Trinidad	200	Water Island	32
Turks and Caicos (U.K.)	10	Venezuela	447
Grand Turk	4	Isla Margarita	1
Middle Caicos	0	Los Roques	0
North Caicos	0	Los Testigos	0

Appendix 11

Map of Properties – Extract Jamaica West, 1768

Extract showing the names of properties including Crooks' Sugar Plantation.

Appendix 12

African Slaves Advertisement

The Royal Gazette, Jamaica, Saturday, 19 January 1793

Appendix 13

Africans Disembarked in the Caribbean, 1776–1800

(1)

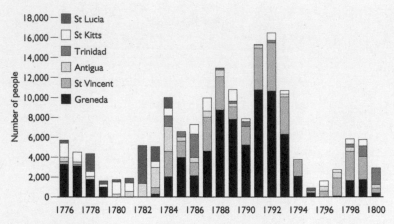

(2)

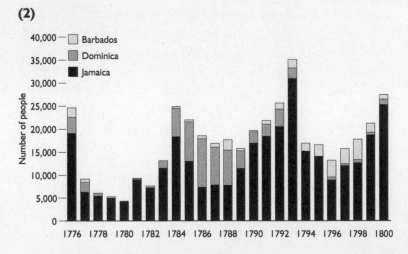

Appendix 14

Extract from the Crooks of Jamaica Website

Sarah Brown and John Alexander Crooks aka 'August'
The family name Crooks is traced along patrilineal lines to John Alexander Crooks, born in West Africa in 1787. Like Ami, he would have arrived prior to 1807, before the trade in Africans was formally abolished.

The 1817 slave register records John's old name August and his Christian name John Alexander Crooks. Baptism register records show that he was baptised on 3 March 1813 with Richard (Dick), an African who was aged fifty-one and William James, a mulatto slave. John Alexander Crooks was one of only a few African (black) Baptists on the estate. A year later, all the slaves of Cousins Cove had been baptised by Anglican Reverend Daniel W. Rose.

Sarah resided within the slave village on the Cousins Cove estate. She would have been a slave in everything but name. Sarah was not listed in the 1817 slave registers. However, in subsequent updates of the register she is listed as the mother of three children, all classified as sambo (of 'mulatto' and 'negro/black' parentage) – John, Barbary, Sam and William. The children's father was John Alexander Crooks – an African. Sarah and John Alexander Crooks never married. Had she done so, the law would have required her to relinquish her free status.

Sarah would have been much younger than John Crooks, who was ten years Ami's junior.

African family units were usually fragmented. Family members – men – were often sold/traded to other property owners and lived away from their loved ones. John Alexander Crooks was an exception. He was at the lowest echelon of slave society. He was African and as such was classified as negro. He was black. He was unskilled and deployed as a field labourer. It was indeed an achievement that his family unit remained intact by the ending of slavery.

At the age of forty-seven, John A. Crooks was one field labourer for whom Neil McCullum, the owner of Cousins Cove Sugar Plantation, submitted a successful claim for compensation. Neil received a total of £10,080. It appears that McCullum won an appeal and in 1836 was awarded an additional £3,799. *The Royal Gazette*, 1934, published details of the proportion of the £20 million compensation fund allotted to Jamaica's slave-owning class.

Slavery was abolished in 1838. The former European owners often refused to sell land to ex-slaves. The intention was to tie the ex-slaves to plantations as low-wage workers. They would seek to charge the ex-slaves rent that would exceed their wages. Some remained on the estates because of their attachment to their homes and provision grounds. Other reasons included the availability of certain services such as medical treatment which was granted free of charge. For some it was better to stay than to escape to an uncertain future. A number of Cousins Cove slaves stayed behind. To this day there is still a clan of Crooks descended from the Cousins Cove community living in Hanover, in and around Cousins Cove.

Many ex-slaves had other plans. It is said that these ex-slaves set out for the mountains as soon as Queen Victoria signed emancipation papers at Frogmore, Windsor. Black people went into the mountains for psychological and economic reasons.

John Alexander Crooks was one who, with his family, abandoned the Cove – heading for the hills and over the Hanover border into Westmoreland to settle at Jerusalem Mountain, in proximity to an old coffee and pimento plantation. The National

Library of Jamaica has no record for Jerusalem/Jerusalem Mountain. There were no surveys of the land logged. Getting legal title to land was a different matter, requiring much time and expense. The plot of land would no doubt have been acquired either by purchase, rental or illegal occupation. If the land was bought, he may well have sought help from the church, i.e. the Baptist ministers, to bargain with lenders and to secure land. The church would have sold land to slaves at affordable prices.

However, the 1840 *Jamaica Almanac* records a John Crooks with fourteen acres of land (see Jamaican Family Search Genealogy Research Library).

Co-operative activity among ex-slaves stimulated the growth of the free villages. Whatever the circumstances, like so many in his position, he would have been attracted towards subsistence peasant agriculture. John may have grown fruit, root vegetables, and sugar for the local market; ginger, pimento, and coffee for the export one.

There is a death record for a Sarah Brown in 1853 in Westmoreland, coinciding with an outbreak of cholera that is believed to have hit parts of Jamaica during this time.

William & Ellen Crooks
William was the youngest child born to Sarah Brown and John Alexander Crooks. William was born into bondage on the Cousins Cove Sugar Plantation in 1832. He and his two surviving siblings (Sam Crooks died after just twenty-eight days) were all baptised together on the same day, 1 January 1834. He would have been four years old in 1838, the year when the slaves of the British colonies were emancipated. William lived most of his life in the hills of Jerusalem Mountain.

Before 1850, almost no attention was paid to the formal education, or even religious instruction of black people in the rural areas of Westmoreland. Jamaica's European settlers were afraid of what a little knowledge could do to unsettle the minds of the former slaves. The early attempts at public education suffered for a number of reasons including a heavy emphasis on religion, insufficient and poorly trained teachers, a scarcity of teaching equipment and inadequate supervision. The religious denominations played a significant role in helping to expand education in Jamaica. Like his father, he became a labourer.

William married Ellen on 1 June 1856. The Reverend Henry Clarke administered the ceremony, and he may well have played an important role in the Westmoreland Crooks' changing fortunes. According to oral accounts Ellen lived 100 years. William and Ellen parented five children. Robert Crooks was the youngest.

For further information, please visit: www.netcomuk.co.uk/~prCrooks/index.html

Resources

This section includes information you may find helpful for tracing your ancestry, and includes a family tree template, useful websites, a list of public records offices in Britain and the Caribbean, a list of Caribbean newspapers available at the British Library, and a list of libraries holding *Lloyd's List* and *Register*.

FAMILY TREE TEMPLATE

FAMILY TREE OF: .... **DATE:**....................

Name .... Date of birth .... Town of birth .... Country	Name .... Date of birth .... Town of birth .... Country	My Great Great Grandparents' story
Name .... Date of birth .... Town of birth .... Country	Name .... Date of birth .... Town of birth .... Country	My Great Grandparents' story (use another sheet of paper)
Name .... Date of birth .... Town of birth .... Country	Name .... Date of birth .... Town of birth .... Country	My Grandparents' story (use another sheet of paper)
Name .... Date of birth .... Town of birth .... Country	Name .... Date of birth .... Town of birth .... Country	My Parents' story (use another sheet of paper)

Name
....
Date of birth
....
Town of birth
....
Country
....

My Life
(use another sheet of paper)

The things I would want my children, and my children's children to know about our Family History
(use another sheet of paper)

For help go to
www.netcomuk.co.uk/~prcrooks

Websites

AfriGeneas www.afrigeneas.com: Afrigeneas is a site devoted to African American genealogy, to researching African ancestry in the Americas in particular and to genealogical research and resources in general. It is also an African ancestry research community featuring the AfriGeneas mail list, the AfriGeneas message boards and daily and weekly genealogy chats.

Rootsweb.com www.rootsweb.ancestry.com: RootsWeb.com is a thriving, free genealogy community on the web, providing a robust worldwide environment for learning, collaborating and sharing for the expert and novice alike.

Ancestry.com www.ancestry.com: With more than 5 billion names and 23,000 searchable databases, Ancestry.com is the number one online source for family history information, including the web's largest collection of historical records.

Genealogy.com www.genealogy.com: Few other family history sites are as trusted or as visited as Genealogy.com, which offers a wide range of family and local histories, vital records, military records and much more.

Barbados - Christ Church Baptisms http://www.rootsweb.ancestry. com/~caribgw/cgw_archive/barbados/baptism1.htm: A detailed archive of the Christian baptisms in seventeenth-century Barbados.

ABC Genealogy http://www.abcgenealogy.com: A regional guide to family history research on the web.

Caribbean Genealogy Research Antigua and the Leeward Islands http://www.candoo.com/genresources/anuleewards.htm: Caribbean Genealogy Research Country Resources about Antigua and the Leeward Islands (register of slaves, court records, history of the island of Antigua, registrar general).

The Bahamas/Bahama Islands GenWeb Project www.rootsweb. ancestry.com/~bhswgw/: Part of the regional Caribbean GenWeb Project, which is part of the World GenWeb Project. On these pages you will find the resources you need to find clues to family ties to these islands.

Haiti Genealogy (Généalogie d'Haiti et de Saint-Domingue de la colonie à la République) www.rootsweb.ancestry.com/~htiwgw/: A study of the genealogy and of the patronymics on the Island of Hispaniola, accompanied by the list of the governors and the presidents of Haiti.

Adoption Resources www.adoptionresources.org: The purpose of Adoption Resources is to serve the best interests of children, so that each child will be raised in a permanent and loving family. Adoption Resources provides services that protect the dignity of children, birth parents, adoptive families, and foster families.

The Genealogy Home Page www.genhomepage.com: Displays every kind of available genealogy resources (websites, libraries, archives, studies…) worldwide.

TreEZy - The Genealogy and History Search Engine www.genealogyportal.com: Provides comprehensive search engines and links to assist you in completing your family history.

RootsWeb Meta Search http://resources.rootsweb.ancestry.com/cgi-bin/metasearch

RootsWeb Surname List http://rsl.rootsweb.ancestry.com

Public Records – Britain and the Caribbean

	The British Library Asia, Pacific and Africa Collections 96 Euston Road London NW1 2DB Tel: +44 (0)20 7412 7873 Fax: +44 (0)20 7412 7641 Email: *oioc-enquiries@bl.uk*
	The Btitish Library Newspapers Colindale Avenue London NW9 5HE Tel: +44 (0)20 7412 7353 Fax: +44 (0)20 7412 7379 Email: *newspaper@bl.uk*
	The British Library Boston Spa Wetherby West Yorkshire LS23 7BQ Tel: +44 (0)870 444 1500
	The National Archives, Kew, Richmond, Surrey, TW9 4DU. Tel: +44 (0) 20 8876 3444
Anguilla	Anguilla Library Service, The Valley, Anguilla, BWI, tel: (264) 497 2441 Registrar of Births, Deaths and Marriages, Judicial Department, The Valley, Anguilla, BWI, tel: (264) 497 2377

Antigua	The National Archives, Rappaport Centre, Victoria Park, St John's Antigua, West Indies, tel: (268) 462 3946, email: *archives@candw.ag* The Registrar General's Office, High Court, High Street, St John's Antigua, West Indies, tel: (268) 462 3929
Bahamas	Department of Archives, PO Box SS-6341, Nassau, Bahamas *www.bahamasnationalarchives.bs* tel: (242) 393 2175, email: archives@batelnet.bs Registrar General's Office, PO Box N532, Nassau, Bahamas, tel: (242) 322 3316
Barbados	Department of Archives, Lazaretto Building, Black Rock, St Michael, Barbados, tel: (246) 425 1380, email: *bda@caribsurf.com* Registration Department, Supreme Court of Barbados, Law Courts, Colleridge St, Bridgetown, Barbados, tel: (246) 426 3461
Belize	Belize Archives Department, 26/28 Unity Boulevard, Belmopan, Belize (*www.belize.gov.bz/ archives_dept/belize*), tel: (501) 8 22247, email: *archives@btl. net* Registrar General, Supreme Court, Belize City, Belize, tel: (501) 2 77377

British Virgin Islands	Library Services Department, Flemming St, Road Town, Tortola, British Virgin Islands, tel: (284) 494 3428 Registrar of Births, Deaths and Marriages, Government of the British Virgin Islands, Central Administration Complex, Road Town, Tortola, British Virgin Islands, tel: (284) 494 3701
Cayman Islands	Cayman Islands National Archive, Government Administration Building, Grand Cayman, Cayman Islands. tel: (345) 949 9809, email: *CINA@gov.ky* Registrar of Births, Deaths and Marriages, General Registry Department, Tower Building, Grand Cayman. tel: (345) 244 3404
Dominica	National Documentation Centre, Government Headquarters, Roseau, Commonwealth of Dominica, tel: (767) 448 2401 General Registrar, Bay Front, Roseau, Commonwealth of Dominica, tel: (767) 448 2401
Grenada	Public Library/National Archives, 2 Carenage, St George's, Grenada, tel: (473) 440 2506 Registrar General, Church St, St George's, Grenada, tel: (473) 440 2030
Guyana	National Archives of Guyana, 26 Main Street, Georgetown, Guyana, tel: (592) 227 7687, email: *narchivesguyana@yahoo.com* General Register Office, GPO Building, Robb Street, Georgetown, Guyana, tel: (592) 225 7561

Jamaica	Jamaica Archives, Spanish Town, Jamaica, tel: (876) 984 2581 The Registrar General, Vital Records Information, Twickenham Park, Spanish Town, Jamaica www.rgd.gov.jm email: information@rgd.gov.jm tel: (876) 984 3041 5
Montserrat	Montserrat Public Library, Government Headquarters, Plymouth, Montserrat, tel: (664) 491 4706, email: publiclibrary@candw.ag Registrar General, PO Box 22, Plymouth, Montserrat, tel: (664) 491 2129
St Kitts and Nevis	National Archives, Government Headquarters, Church St, Box 186,Basseterre, St Kitts, West Indies, tel: (869) 465 2521 Nevis Archives and Library, Nevis Historical and Conservation Society, Nelson Museum, Bellevue, Charlestown, Nevis, West Indies, tel: (869) 469 0408, email: archives-library@nevis-nhcs.org Registrar General, PO Box 236, Basseterre, St Kitts, West Indies, tel: (869) 465 5251
St Lucia	St Lucia National Archives, PO Box 3060, Clarke St, Vigie, Castries, St Lucia, tel: (758) 452 1654, email: stlunatarch_mt@candw.lc Registrar of Civil Status, Peynier Street, Castries, St Lucia, tel: (758) 452 1257

St Vincent and the Grenadines	Archives Department, Cotton Ginnery Compound, Frenches, Kingstown, St Vincent and the Grenadines, tel: (784) 456 1689, email: *document@caribsurf.com*
	Registrar General, Government Buildings, Kingstown, St Vincent and the Grenadines, tel: (784) 457 1424
Trinidad and Tobago	National Archives, PO Box 763, 105 St Vincent St, Port-of-Spain, Trinidad, tel: (868) 625 2689 Registrar General's Office, Registration House, South Quay, Port-of-Spain, Trinidad, tel: (868) 623 2450
	Tobago Registrar General's Office, Jerningham Street, Scarborough, Tobago, tel: (868) 639 3210

Family History Centres in England

Aldershot England
St. Georges Road
Aldershot, Hampshire, England
Phone: 1252-321460

Ashton England
Patterdale Road Crowhill Estate
Ashton-under-Lyne, Lancashire,
    England
Phone: 161-330-3453

Barrow England
Abbey Road
Barrow-In-Furness, Cumbria, England
Phone: 44-1229-820050

Billingham England
The Linkway
Billingham, Cleveland, England
Phone: 44-1642-563162

Blackpool England
Warren Drive, Cleveleys
Blackpool, Lancashire, England
Phone: 44-1253-858218

Boston England
Woodthorpe Avenue
Fishtoft
Boston, Lincolnshire, England
Phone: 44-1522-680117

Bristol England
721 Wells Road
Whitchurch
Bristol, Somerset, England
Phone: 1275-838326
Hours: M–W, F–Sat 10am–4pm;
    F 7pm–9.30pm. Saturdays by
    appointment only

Cambridge England
670 Cherry Hinton Road
Cambridge, Cambridgeshire, England
Phone: 1223-247010

Canterbury England
Forty Acres Road
Canterbury, Kent, England
Phone: 44-1227-765431

Carlisle England
Langrigg Road
Morton Park
Carlisle, Cumbria, England
Phone: 1228-526767
Hours: T–W 9.30am–2pm; W
  7pm–9pm

Cheltenham England
Thirlestaine Road
Cheltenham, Gloucesteshire, England
Phone: 44-1242-523433.

Coventry England
Riverside Close
Whitley
Coventry, West Midlands, England
Phone: 24-7630-3316

Crawley England
Old Horsham Road
Crawley, West Sussex, England
Phone: 1293-516151

Dereham England
Yaxham Road
East Dereham, Norfolk, England
Phone: 01362 851500
Hours: T–Th 6pm–9pm

Douglas Isle of Man
Woodside-Woodburn Road
Douglas, Isle of Man, England
Phone: 44-1624-675834

Exeter England
Wonford Road
Off Barrack Road
Exeter, Devon, England
Phone: 44-1392-250723

Forest of Dean England
Wynols Hill
Queensway
Colesford, Gloucestershire, England
Phone: 1594-832904

Gillingham England
2 Twydall Lane
Gillingham, Kent, England
Phone: 44-1634-388900

Grimsby England
Linwood Avenue
Waltham Road
Grimsby, Lincolnshire, England
Phone: 1472-828876

Harborne England
38-42 Lordswood Road
Harborne, Birmingham, England
Phone: 44-121-427-6858

Hastings England
2 Ledsham Avenue
St. Leonards-on-Sea, East Sussex,
  England
Phone: 1424-754563

Helston England
Clodgey Lane
Helston, Cornwall, England
Phone: 1326-564503

High Wycombe England
743 London Road
High Wycombe, Buckinghamshire,
  England
Phone: 1494-459979

Huddersfield England
12 Halifax Road
Birchencliffe
Huddersfield, West Yorkshire, England
Phone: 1484-454573

Hull England
727 Holderness Road
Hull, Yorkshire, England
Phone: 44-1482-701439

Ipswich England
42 Sidegate Lane West
Ipswich, Suffolk, England
Phone: 44-1473-723182

Kings Lynn England
Reffley Lane
Kings Lynn, Norfolk, England
Phone: 1553-670000

Lancaster England
Overangle Road
Lancaster, Lancashire, England
Phone: 1524-33571

Leeds England
Vesper Road
Hacksworth
Leeds, West Yorkshire, England
Phone: 113-258-5297

Leicester England
Wakerley Road
Leicester, Leicestershire, England
Phone: 116-249-0099

Lichfield England
Purcell Avenue
Lichfield, Staffordshire, England
Phone: 1543-414843

Lincoln England
Skellingthorpe Road
Lincoln, Lincolnshire, England

Liverpool England
4 Mill Bank
West Derby
Liverpool, Merseyside, England

London England Hyde Park
64-68 Exhibition Road
London, Greater London, England
Phone: 20-7589-8561

London England Wandsworth
149 Nightingale Lane
Balham
London, Greater London, England

Lowestoft England
165 Yarmouth Road
Lowestoft, Suffolk, England

Macclesfield England
Victoria Road
Macclesfield, Cheshire, England
Phone: 44-1625-427236

Maidstone England
76B London Road
Maidstone, Kent, England
Phone: 1622-757811

Manchester England
Altrincham Road
Wythenshawe
Manchester, Lancashire, England
Phone: 44-161-902-9279

Mansfield England
Southridge Drive
Mansfield, Nottinghamshire, England
Phone: 01623 662333

Newcastle-Under-Lyme England
The Brampton
Newcastle-Under-Lyme,
Staffordshire, England
Phone: 44-1782-630178

Newport England
Chestnut Close
Shide Road
Newport, Isle of Wight, England
Phone: 1983-532833

Northampton England
137 Harlestone Road
Northampton, Northamptonshire,
England
Phone: 44-160-458-7630

Norwich England
19 Greenways
Norwich, Norfolk, England
Phone: 44-1603-452440

Nottingham England
Stanhome Square
West Bridgford
Nottingham, Nottinghamshire,
England
Phone: 44-0115 923 3856

Orpington England
Station Approach
Orpington, Kent, England
Phone: 1689-837342

Peterborough England
Cottesmore Close, off Atherstone
Ave
Netherton Estate
Peterborough, Cambridgeshire,
England
Phone: 1733-263374

Plymouth England
Mannamead Road
Hartley
Plymouth, Devon, England
Phone: 01752-668666

Pontefract England
Park Villas Drive
Pontefract, West Yorkshire, England
Phone: 1977-600308

Poole England
8 Mount Road
Parkstone
Poole, Dorset, England
Phone: 1202-730646

Portsmouth England
Kingston Crescent
Portsmouth, Hampshire, England
Phone: 23-9269-6243

Preston England
Temple Way
Hartwood Green
Chorley, Lancashire, England
Phone: 44-1257-226145

Rawtenstall England
Haslingden New Road
Rawtenstall, Lancashire, England
Phone: 44-1282-412748

Reading England
280, The Meadway
Tilehurst
Reading, Berkshre, England
Phone: 44-118-941-0211

Redditch England
321 Evesham Road
Crabbs Cross
Redditch, Worcestershire, England
Phone: 1527-401543

Romford England
64 Butts Green Road
Hornchurch, Essex, England
Phone: 1708-620727

Scarborough England
Stepney Road
Scarborough
North Humberside, North Yorkshire,
  England
Phone: 44-1723-501026

Sheffield England
Wheel Lane
Grenoside
Sheffield, Yorkshire, England
Phone: 114-245-3124

St Albans England
Cutenhoe Road
Luton, Bedfordshire, England
Phone: 1582-482234

St Austell England
Kingfisher Drive
St Austell, Cornwall, England
Phone: 44-1726-69912

Staines England
41 Kingston Road
Staines, Middlesex, England
Phone: 44-1784-462627

Stevenage England
Buckthorne Avenue
Stevenage, Hertfordshire, England
Phone: 44-1438-351553

Sunderland England
Queen Alexandra Road
Sunderland, Tyne & Wear, England
Phone: 44-191-528-5787

Sutton Coldfield England
187 Penns Lane
Sutton Coldfield, West Midlands,
  England
Phone: 44-121-386-4902

Telford England
72 Glebe Street
Wellington, Shropshire, England
Phone: 1952-257443

Thetford England
Station Road
Thetford, Norfolk, England
Phone: 1842-755472

Trowbridge England
Brook Road
Trowbridge, Wiltshire, England
Phone: 1225-777097

Watford England
Hempstead Road
Watford, Hertfordshire, England
Phone: 44-1923-251471

Wednesfield England
Linthouse Lane
Wednesfield
Wolverhampton, West Midlands,
  England
Phone: 44-1902-724097

Weymouth England
396 Chickerell Road
Weymouth, Dorset, England.

Worcester England
Canada Way
Lower Wick
Worcester, Worcestershire, England
Phone: 44-1905-420341

Worthing England
Goring Street
Worthing, West Sussex, England
Phone: 01903 241829

Yate England
Wellington Road
Yate, Avon, England
Phone: 1454-323004

Yeovil England
Lysander Road
Forest Hill, Somerset, England
Phone: 44-1935-426817

York England
West Bank
Acomb
York, Yorkshire, England
Phone: 1904-786784

Family History Centres in Scotland

Aberdeen Scotland
North Anderson Drive
Aberdeen, Grampian, Scotland
Phone: 44-1224-692206

Alloa Scotland
Grange Road
Westend Park
Alloa, Central, Scotland
Phone: 44-1259-211148

Ayr Scotland
Corner of Orchard Ave & Mossgiel
    Road
Ayr, Ayrshire, Scotland

Dumfries Scotland
36 Edinburgh Road
Albanybank
Dumfries, Dumfrieshire, Scotland
Phone: 44-1387-254865

Dundee Scotland
Bingham Terrace
Dundee, Tayside, Scotland
Phone: 1382-451247

Edinburgh Scotland
30A Colinton Road
Edinburgh, Lothian, Scotland
Phone: 44-131-313-2762

Elgin Scotland
Pansport Road
Elgin, Morayshire, Scotland
Phone: 1343-546429

Glasgow Scotland
35 Julian Avenue
Kelvinside
Glasgow, Scotland
Phone: 44-141-357-1024

Invergordon Scotland
Kilmonivaig Seafield
Portmahomack, Ross-shire, Scotland
Phone: 44-1862-871631

Inverness Scotland
13 Ness Walk
Inverness, Inverness-shire, Scotland
Phone: 1463-231220

Kirkcaldy Scotland
Winifred Crescent
Forth Park
Kirkcaldy, Fifeshire, Scotland
Phone: 1592-640041

Lerwick Scotland
44 Prince Alfred Street
Lerwick, Shetland, Shetland Islands,
    Scotland
Phone: 1595-695732

Montrose Scotland
LDS Chapel
Coronation Way
Montrose, Angus, Tayside, Scotland

Paisley Scotland
Glenburn Road
Paisley, Renfrewshire, Scotland
Phone: 141-884-2780

Stornoway Scotland
Newton Street
Stornoway, Isle of Lewis, Scotland
Phone: 1851-870972

Family History Centres in Wales

Cardiff Wales
Heol-Y-Deri
Cardiff, South Glamorgan, Wales
Phone: 44-2920-625342

Chester England
Aled House
Lakeside Business Village
St David's Park, Flintshire, Wales
Phone: 01244 538356

Cwmbran Wales
Lds Chapel,
The Highway, Croesceiliog
Cwmbran, Gwent, Wales
Phone: 44-1633-483-856

Gaerwen Wales
Holyhead Road
Gaerwen, Anglesey, Wales
Phone: 44-1248-421-894

Merthyr Tydfil Wales
Nantygwenith Street
Merthyr Tydfil, Mid Glamorgan, Wales
Phone: 44-1685-722455

Newcastle Emlyn Wales
Cardigan Road
Newcastle Emlyn, Dyfed, Wales
Phone: 1239-711472

Rhyl Wales
171 Vale Road
Rhyl, Denbighshire, Wales
Phone: 44-1745-331172

Swansea Wales
Cockett Road
Cockett
Swansea, West Glamorgan, Wales
Phone: 44-1792-585792

Family History Centres in Northern Ireland

Belfast Northern Ireland
403 Holywood Road
Belfast, Down, Northern Ireland
Phone: 28-9076 9839

Coleraine Northern Ireland
8 Sandelfields
Knocklynn Road
Coleraine, Londonderry, Northern
Ireland
Phone: 44-2870-321214

Londonderry Northern Ireland
Racecourse Road
Belmont Estate
Londonderry, Northern Ireland
Phone: 44-28-7135-0179

Family History Centres in Ireland

Cork Ireland
Sarsfield Road
Wilton
Cork, Ireland
Phone: 353-21-4897050

Dublin Ireland
Finglas Road
Glasnevin
Dublin, Ireland

Limerick Ireland
Doradoyle Road
Limerick, Ireland
Phone: 353-61-309-443

Caribbean Newspapers
The following newspapers may be found at the British Library.

Caribbean

Caribbean Business News   Toronto, Ontario, Canada, 1969–1970

Caribbean Times   London, England, 1965–1965

Caribbean Times   London, England, 1981 to date

Magnet	The voice of the Afro-Asian Caribbean peoples, London, England, 1965–1965
North Caribbean Star (The)	[Armed Forces Newspapers], England, 1945–1946
Panama Times	South Seas and Caribbean Mail, Panama City, Panama, 1925–1928
Platform	London, England, 1987 to date
St. Christopher Gazette, and Caribbean Courier (The)	Basseterre, Saint Christopher, Saint Christopher - Nevis, 1837–1909
Weekly Journal (The)	London, England, 1996–1997

Jamaica

AIRS Index to the Daily Gleaner	Kingston; Jamaica, 1975–1984
Budget (The)	Kingston; Jamaica, 1877–1886
Church Notes A Church of England newspaper	Kingston; Jamaica, 1903–1904
Colonial Reformer (The)	Spanish Town; Jamaica, 1839–1841
Colonial Standard (The)	Kingston; Jamaica, 1850–1850
Colonial Standard and Jamaica Despatch (The)	Kingston; Jamaica, 1850–1895
Colonial Union	Kingston; Jamaica, 1831–1831
Cornwall Chronicle & General Advertiser (The)	Montego Bay; Jamaica, 1776–1777
Cornwall Chronicle and County Gazette	Montego Bay; Jamaica, 1839–1839
Cornwall Chronicle and Jamaica General Advertizer (The)	Montego Bay; Jamaica, 1781–1794
Cornwall Courier, and Jamaica General Intelligencer	Falmouth; Jamaica, 1839–1839
County Union (The)	Montego Bay; Jamaica, 1864–1864

County Union and Anglo–Jamaican Advertizer (The)	Montego Bay; Jamaica, 1865–1874
Daily Advertiser	Kingston; Jamaica, 1790–1790
Daily Advertiser and Lawton's Commercial Gazette (The)	Kingston; Jamaica, 1858–1858
Daily Chronicle	Kingston; Jamaica, 1914–1917
Daily Gleaner (The)	Kingston; Jamaica, 1902 to date
Daily Gleaner and De Cordova's Advertising Sheet (The)	Kingston; Jamaica, 1879–1902
Daily Telegraph and Jamaica Guardian (The)	Kingston; Jamaica, 1911–1912
Evening Budget (The)	Kingston; Jamaica, 1887–1888
Evening Express (The)	Kingston; Jamaica, 1884–1888
Falmouth Gazette and Jamaica General Advertiser (The)	Falmouth; Jamaica, 1879–1888
Falmouth Post and Jamaica General Advertiser (The)	Falmouth; Jamaica, 1839–1877
Gall's "Packet" News Letter	Kingston; Jamaica, 1873–1899
Gleaner (The)	Kingston; Jamaica, 1987–1995
Gleaner (The) Packet ed.	Kingston; Jamaica, 1874–1891
Gleaner Index (The)	Kingston; Jamaica, 1986 to date
Gleaner and De Cordova's Advertising Sheet (The)	Kingston; Jamaica, 1866–1874
Jamaica Baptist Reporter	Kingston; Jamaica, 1884–1884
Jamaica Christian Chronicle (The)	Kingston; Jamaica, 1888–1894
Jamaica Churchman (The)	Kingston; Jamaica, 1899–1915
Jamaica Courant	Kingston; Jamaica, 1832–1832
Jamaica Courant	Kingston; Jamaica, 1833–1833
Jamaica Courant and Public Advertiser	Kingston; Jamaica, 1827–1831
Jamaica Creole (The)	Kingston; Jamaica, 1878–1879
Jamaica Creole and Daily Record (The)	Kingston; Jamaica, 1882–1883

Jamaica Daily News (The)	Kingston; Jamaica, 1980–1983
Jamaica Daily Telegraph and Anglo–American Herald	Kingston; Jamaica, 1899–1909
Jamaica Despatch and Shannon's Daily Messenger	Kingston; Jamaica, 1834–1834
Jamaica Despatch, and Jamaica Gazette	Kingston; Jamaica, 1840–1840
Jamaica Despatch, and Kingston Chronicle	Kingston; Jamaica, 1838–1839
Jamaica Despatch, and New Courant	Kingston; Jamaica, 1836–1838
Jamaica Despatch, and New Courant	Kingston; Jamaica, 1836–1838
Jamaica Exports	Kingston; Jamaica, 1979–1981
Jamaica Gazette	Kingston; Jamaica, 1838–1839
Jamaica Gleaner (The) Overseas edition	Kingston; Jamaica, 1960–1961
Jamaica Guardian (The)	Kingston; Jamaica, 1864–1871
Jamaica Instructor (The)	Kingston; Jamaica, 1872–1879

Barbados

Advocate (The) (Home edition.)	Bridgetown; Barbados, 1961–1968
Advocate News	Bridgetown; Barbados, 1968–1987
Barbadian (The)	Bridgetown; Barbados, 1822–1861
Barbadian (The)	Bridgetown; Barbados, 1839–1840
Barbados Advocate [Daily edition.]	Bridgetown; Barbados, 1926–1961
Barbados Agricultural Gazette and Planters' Journal	Bridgetown; Barbados, 1884–1887
Barbados Agricultural Reporter (The)	Bridgetown; Barbados, 1870–1922
Barbados Agricultural Reporter, and Planter's Scientific Journal (The)	Bridgetown; Barbados, 1845–1846

Barbados Daily News	Bridgetown; Barbados, 1960–1963
Barbados Daily News	Bridgetown; Barbados, 1967–1967
Barbados Gazette, or, General Intelligencer (The)	Bridgetown; Barbados, 1787–1789
Barbados Globe and Colonial Advocate	Bridgetown; Barbados, 1837–1926
Barbados Herald	Bridgetown; Barbados, 1879–1896
Barbados Mercury	Bridgetown; Barbados, 1783–1789
Barbados Mercury, and Bridge–town Gazette	Bridgetown; Barbados, 1805–1824
Barbados Mercury, and Bridge–town Gazette	Bridgetown; Barbados, 1839–1840
Barbados Observer	Bridgetown; Barbados, 1958–1966
Barbados People, and Windward Islands Gazette (The)	Bridgetown; Barbados, 1876–1876
Barbados Recorder (The)	Bridgetown; Barbados, 1951–1959
Barbados Standard (The)	Bridgetown; Barbados, 1911–1921
Barbados Times (The)	Bridgetown; Barbados, 1920–1921
Beacon (The)The paper of the Barbados Labour Party and of the Barbados Workers' Union	Bridgetown; Barbados, 1958–1966
Daily News (The)	Bridgetown; Barbados, 1963–1966
Liberal (The)	Bridgetown; Barbados, 1839–1840
Liberal (The) (Mail edition.)	Bridgetown; Barbados, 1864–1864
New Times (The)	Bridgetown; Barbados, 1839–1839
Sun (The)	Bridgetown; Barbados, 1840–1840
Times (The)	Bridgetown; Barbados, 1863–1895
Torch (The)	Bridgetown; Barbados, 1958–1960
Truth	Bridgetown; Barbados, 1960–1966
Weekly Illustrated Paper (The)	Bridgetown; Barbados, 1919–1921
Weekly Recorder (The)	Bridgetown; Barbados, 1897–1910
West Indian	Bridgetown; Barbados, 1839–1885

Antigua

Antigua Herald and Gazette;	Saint John's Antigua, 1839–1848
Antigua Magnet (The)	Saint John's Antigua, 1930–1940
Antigua New Era (The);	Saint John's Antigua, 1874–1875
Antigua News Notes;	Saint John's Antigua, 1909–1911
Antigua Observer (The);	Saint John's Antigua, 1848–1903
Antigua Standard (The	Saint John's Antigua, 1883–1908
Antigua Star (The);	Saint John's Antigua, 1937–1940
Antigua Times (The);	Saint John's Antigua, 1863–1883
Antigua Times (The);	Saint John's Antigua, 1897–1899
Antigua Weekly Register (The)	Saint John's Antigua, 1848–1882
New Era (The);	Saint John's Antigua, 1881–1883
Record (The);	Saint John's Antigua, 1887–1888
Sun (The);	Saint John's Antigua, 1911–1920
Weekly Register (The);	Saint John's Antigua, 1838–1840
Workers' Voice;	Saint John's Antigua, 1970–1971

St Kitts

St. Kitts Commercial News	Basseterre Saint Christopher Saint Christopher – Nevis, 1888–1888
St. Kitts Daily Express	Basseterre Saint Christopher Saint Christopher – Nevis, 1884–1915
St. Kitts News–Letter	Basseterre Saint Christopher Saint Christopher – Nevis, 1875–1875
St. Kitts News–Letter	Basseterre Saint Christopher Saint Christopher – Nevis, 1887–1887
St. Kitts–Nevis Daily Bulletin (The)	Basseterre Saint Christopher Saint Christopher – Nevis, 1930–1967
West Indian Weekly Herald and St.Kitts Chronicle (The)	(The West Indian Weekly Herald.) Basseterre Saint Christopher Saint Christopher – Nevis, 1881–1881

St Lucia

St. Lucia Observer (The)	Castries Saint Lucia, 1874–1876
St. Lucian (The)	Castries Saint Lucia, 1863–1873
Voice of St. Lucia (The)	Castries Saint Lucia, 1885–1984

Grenada

Chronicle and Gazette (The)	Saint George's Grenada, 1912–1915
Citizen's Weekly (The)	Saint George's Grenada, 1959–1961
Citizen's Weekly (The)	Saint George's Grenada, 1960–1961
Daily Tidings	Saint George's Grenada, 1886–1886
Equilibrium (The)	Saint George's Grenada, 1882–1887
Excelsior!	Saint George's Grenada, 1876–1876
Federalist (The)	Saint George's Grenada, 1896–1901
Federalist (The)	Saint George's Grenada, 1907–1908
Federalist and Grenada People (The)	Saint George's Grenada, 1901–1907
Federalist and Grenada People (The)	Saint George's Grenada, 1909–1920
Grenada Free Press and Public Gazette (The)	Saint George's Grenada, 1839–1840
Grenada Guardian (The)	Saint George's Grenada, 1930–1935
Grenada People (The)	Saint George's Grenada, 1883–1908
Grenada Phoenix (The)	Saint George's Grenada, 1864–1865
Grenada Reporter (The)	Saint George's Grenada, 1867–1867
New Era (The)	Saint George's Grenada, 1878–1880
St. George's Chronicle and Grenada Gazette (The)	Saint George's Grenada, 1839–1907
Star (The)	Saint George's Grenada, 1962–1962
Torchlight (The)	Saint George's Grenada, 1962–1967
Vanguard (The)	The voice of the Grenada National Party Saint George's Grenada, 1959–1960
Weekly Record (The)	Saint George's Grenada, 1865–1865

West Indian (The)	Saint George's Grenada, 1915–1970
West Indian (The)	Mail edition Saint George's Grenada, 1917–1920

Nevis

Democrat (The)	Basseterre Saint Christopher Saint Christopher – Nevis, 1959–1979
Labour Spokesman (The)	Basseterre Saint Christopher Saint Christopher – Nevis, 1958–1967
Liberal (The)	Charlestown Nevis Saint Christopher – Nevis, 1873–1873
Nevis Guardian (The)	Charlestown Nevis Saint Christopher – Nevis, 1871–1873
Nevis Weekly Recorder	Charlestown Nevis Saint Christopher – Nevis, 1959–1960
Saint Christopher Advertiser and Weekly Intelligencer (The)	Basseterre Saint Christopher Saint Christopher – Nevis, 1839–1909
St. Christopher Gazette, and Caribbean Courier (The)	Basseterre Saint Christopher Saint Christopher – Nevis, 1837–1909
St. Christopher Gazette, or, The Historical Chronicle (The)	Basseterre Saint Christopher Saint Christopher – Nevis, 1771–1771
St. Christopher Independent	Basseterre Saint Christopher Saint Christopher – Nevis, 1882–1886
St. Kitts Commercial News	Basseterre Saint Christopher Saint Christopher – Nevis, 1888–1888
St. Kitts Daily Express	Basseterre Saint Christopher Saint Christopher – Nevis, 1884–1915
St. Kitts News–Letter	Basseterre Saint Christopher Saint Christopher – Nevis, 1875–1875
St. Kitts News–Letter	Basseterre Saint Christopher Saint Christopher – Nevis, 1887–1887
St. Kitts–Nevis Daily Bulletin (The)	Basseterre Saint Christopher Saint Christopher – Nevis, 1930–1967

Union Messenger (The)	Basseterre Saint Christopher Saint Christopher – Nevis, 1930–1961
Voice of the People (The)	Basseterre Saint Christopher Saint Christopher – Nevis, 1875–1880
West Indian Weekly Herald and St.Kitts Chronicle (The)	(The West Indian Weekly Herald.) Basseterre Saint Christopher Saint Christopher – Nevis, 1881–1881

Trinidad

Carindex	Social sciences Saint Augustine Trinidad, 1977 to date
Catholic News (The)	Port Of Spain Trinidad, 1959–1962
Daily Commercial Budget of "Public Opinion" (The)	Port Of Spain Trinidad, 1887–1888
Daily News (The)	Port Of Spain Trinidad, 1896–1896
Echo of Trinidad (The)	Port Of Spain Trinidad, 1870–1873
Evening News	Port Of Spain Trinidad, 1951–1964
Fair Play	Port Of Spain Trinidad, 1874–1875
Fair Play and Trinidad News	Port Of Spain Trinidad, 1878–1884
Fair Play and Trinidad and Venezuelan News	Port of Spain Trinidad, 1877–1878
Independence Times	Port Of Spain Trinidad, 1962–1962
Labour Leader (The)	Port Of Spain Trinidad, 1930–1931
Mirror (The)	Port Of Spain Trinidad, 1898–1916
Moko	Official organ of the United National Independence Party Port Of Spain Trinidad, 1971–1971
Nation (The)	Port Of Spain Trinidad, 1958–1970
New Beginning	Co–ordinating Council news service – Trinidad & Tobago Tunapuna Trinidad, 1971–1971
New Era (The)	Port Of Spain Trinidad, 1869–1891
Port of Spain Gazette (The)	Port Of Spain Trinidad, 1825–1956

Public Opinion	Port Of Spain Trinidad, 1884–1888
Review (The)	Port Of Spain Trinidad, 1869–1870
San Fernando Gazette, and Naparima Agricultural and Commercial Advertiser (The)	San Fernando Trinidad, 1866–1888
Star of the West (The)	Port Of Spain Trinidad, 1864–1874
Statesman (The)	Port Of Spain Trinidad, 1961–1962
Sun (The)	Port Of Spain Trinidad, 1960–1960
Sunday Guardian: The West Indies Federation supplement	Port Of Spain Trinidad, 1958–1958
Telegraph (The)	Port Of Spain Trinidad, 1871–1872
Trinidad Chronicle (The)	Port Of Spain Trinidad, 1864–1885
Trinidad Chronicle and Port of Spain Gazette	Port Of Spain Trinidad, 1956–1959
Trinidad Gazette (The)	Port Of Spain Trinidad, 1820–1822
Trinidad Guardian (The)	Port Of Spain Trinidad, 1917–1988
Trinidad Home Magazine (The)	Port Of Spain Trinidad, 1909–1909
Trinidad News (The)	Port Of Spain Trinidad, 1874–1874
Trinidad Palladium (The)	Port Of Spain Trinidad, 1877–1883
Trinidad Recorder	Port Of Spain Trinidad, 1884–1884
Trinidad Review (The)	Port Of Spain Trinidad, 1884–1884
Trinidad Semi–Monthly Market Report	Port Of Spain Trinidad, 1888–1888
Trinidad Sentinel (The)	Port Of Spain Trinidad, 1856–1864
Trinidad Standard and West Indian Journal	Port Of Spain Trinidad, 1839–1840
Venezolano (El)	Port Of Spain Trinidad, 1886–1888

British Guyana

Commercial Review (The)	British Empire exhibition number Georgetown Guyana, 1924–1924
Royal Gazette of British Guyana	Georgetown Guyana, 1838–1840

Lloyd's List

Lloyd's List is a shipping news journal, and is one of the oldest newspapers still in circulation today. The *Register* provides information on ships. The following are a list of libraries that hold *Lloyd's Register* and *List*.

Library / Institution	Lloyd's Register	Lloyd's List
ABERDEEN		
City of Aberdeen Library Services Rosemount Viaduct Aberdeen AB9 1GU Tel: 01224 652512 Fax: 01224 624118 Email: refloc@arts–rec.aberdeen.net.uk	1934–1952, 1954– 1956/57, 1961/62, 1971–to date	1990–to date (back issues retained for 5 years only)
Aberdeen Maritime Museum Lloyd's Register Library Shiprow Aberdeen AB11 5BY Tel: 01224 337700 Email: info@aagm.co.uk Website: www.aagm.co.uk	1839–1980, incomplete	
BELFAST		
Ulster Folk & Transport Museum The Library Cultra Holywood Co. Down BT18 0EU Tel: 02890 428428 Fax: 02890 428728 Email: uftm@talk21.com Website: www.nidex.com/uftm	1764–to date, incomplete	1741–1826

Library / Institution	Lloyd's Register	Lloyd's List
BIRMINGHAM		
Birmingham Library Services Central Library Chamberlain Square Birmingham B3 3HQ Tel: 0121 303 2751 Fax: 0121 233 4458 Email: bham.socialscience@dial.pipex.com Website: www.birmingham.sou.uk	1834–1872, 1919–1920, 1937–to date	1990 to date (back issues retained for 5 years)
BRISTOL		
Bristol Central Library College Green Bristol Tel: 0117 9299147 Email: refandinfo@bristol–city.gov.uk Website: www.bristol–city.gov.uk		
CARDIFF		
Welsh Industrial & Maritime Museum Cardiff Bay Bute Street Cardiff CF1 6AN Tel: 02920 382116 Fax: 02920 871599 Email: enquiry@libraries.gov.uk Website: www.libraries.cardiff.gov.uk		
CORNWALL		
National Maritime Museum Cornwall Discovery Quay Falmouth Cornwall TR11 3QY Tel: 01326 313388 Fax: 01326 317878 Website: www.nmmc.co.uk	1920–to date	Current year only

Library / Institution	Lloyd's Register	Lloyd's List
The Courtney Library The Royal Institution of Cornwall River Street Truro TRI IHN Tel: 01872 272205 Fax: 01872 240514 Email: courtney.rcmric@btinternet.com Website: www.cornwall–online.co.uk/ric	1894, 1919/20, 1924/25, 1933–35, 1945/46, 1948/49, 1953/54, 1955/56, 1961–66, 1967/68, 1976/77, 1980/81, 1985/86	
DUNDEE		
Dundee District Libraries The Wellgate Dundee DD1 1DB Tel: 01382 434377 Fax: 01382 434642	1885, 1887–88, 1891, 1893, 1898, 1913–18, 1935, 1937–43, 1946, 1950–52, 1955, 1957–59, 1961–62, 1968–70, 1972–73, 1975–80, 1982, 1985–89, 1991–95	Current year only
EDINBURGH		
Edinburgh City Libraries Central Reference Library George IV Bridge Edinburgh EH1 1EG Tel: 0131 2428060 Fax: 0131 2428009 Email: central.reference.library@edinburgh.gov.uk	1896–to date	Current year only

Library / Institution	Lloyd's Register	Lloyd's List
National Library of Scotland Main Library George IV Bridge Edinburgh EHI IEG Tel: 0131 2264531 Fax: 0131 6224803 Email: enquiries@nls.uk Website: www.nls.uk	1896–to date	1785–to date (1838–1926 microfilm)
EXETER		
Devon Library Services Exeter Central Library Castle Street Exeter Devon EX4 3PQ	1856, 1946– 48, 1950–55, 1958–63, 1965–66, 1968–82, 1984–to date	Current year only
GLASGOW		
Archives Services University of Glasgow 13 Thurso Street Glasgow GII 6PE Tel: 0141 330 5515 Fax: 0141 330 2640 Website: www.archives.gla.ac.uk	1834– 1975/76, 1977/78– 1986/87, 1989/90– 1991/92	
The Mitchell Library Glasgow City Library North Street Glasgow G3 7DW Tel: 0141 287 2865 Fax: 0141 287 2871 Email: margaret.wallace@gcl.glasgow.gov.uk	1764, 1768, 1776, 1778– 84, 1786–87, 1789–1816, 1818–to date	1896–1934, 1987–to date

Library / Institution	Lloyd's Register	Lloyd's List
GRIMSBY		
Grimsby Central Reference Library Town Hall Square Great Grimsby South Humberside DN31 1HG Tel: 01472 323600	1764, 1768, 1776, 1778–84, 1786–87, 1789–1816, 1818–1902, 1906–08, 1910–to date	Current year only
GWYNEDD		
Meirionnydd Record Office Cae Penarlag Dolgellau Gwynedd LL40 2YB Tel: 01341 424443 Fax: 01341 424505 Email: archives.dolgellau@gwynedd.gov.uk	1872, 1886, 1900–01, 1910–11, 1915–17, 1924–33	
HULL		
Hull Central Library Albion Street Hull HU1 3TF Tel: 01482 210055	1764, 1768, 1776, 1778–84, 1786–1816, 1818–89, 1890–1900, 1904/5, 1909/10, 1914–17, 1918/19–1920/21, 1924–to date	Current year only

Library / Institution	Lloyd's Register	Lloyd's List
LEEDS		
Leeds Central Library Municipal Buildings Calverley Street Leeds LS1 3AB Tel: 0113 2478274 Fax: 0113 2478271	1914/15 (Vol. 1), 1928/29, 1931/32, 1934/35 (Vol. 2), 1943/44, 1946/47, 1948–50, 1952/53, 1954/55, 1956/57, 1958/59, 1960/61, 1962–67, 1968/69, 1970/71, 1972/73, 1974–to date	
LONDON		
Guildhall Library Aldermanbury London EC2P 2EJ Tel: 020 73321863 Fax: 020 76003384 Email: manuscripts.guildhall@ ms.corpoflondon.gov.uk Website: www.ihr.sas.ac.uk/ihr/ghmnu.html	1764–66, 1768–to date	1741 to date
Lloyd's Register of Shipping 71 Fenchurch Street London EC3M 4BS Tel: 020 7709 9166 Fax: 020 7488 4796 Email: lloydsreg@ir.org Website: www.ir.org	1764–to date	

Library / Institution	Lloyd's Register	Lloyd's List
National Maritime Museum Caird Library Park Row Greenwich London SE10 9NF Tel: 020 83126528 Email: library@nmm.ac.uk Website: www.nmm.ac.uk	1764–85, 1794–1833, 1836–86, 1888–to date	1741–to date
Tower Hamlets Local History Library Bancroft Library 277 Bancroft Road London E1 4DQ Tel: 020 8980 4366 Fax: 020 8983 4510	1842/43, 1844/45, 1851/52, 1857/58, 1861/62, 1863/64, 1866–68, 1869/70, 1876–79, 1880/81, 1884/85, 1890–92, 1894–96, 1897–99, 1911/12, 1918/19, 1920/21, 1926/27, 1932/33, 1935–39, 1941/42, 1944/45, 1954/55–75, 1977/78–79	

Library / Institution	Lloyd's Register	Lloyd's List
MANCHESTER		
Manchester Central Library St. Peter's Square Manchester M2 5PD Tel: 0161 234 1900 Email: mclib@libraries.manchester.gov.uk	1925, 1963, 1995/96	Current year only
MIDDLESBOROUGH		
Middlesborough Group Library Victoria Square Middlesborough TS1 2AY Tel: 01642 263358 Fax: 01642 263354	1835–to date	
NEWCASTLE UPON TYNE		
Newcastle Libraries and Information Service City Library Princess Square Newcastle upon Tyne NE99 1DX Tel: 0191 277 4100 Fax: 0191 277 4137	1764, 1768, 1776–84, 1786–87, 1789–1816, 1818–1900, 1907–37, 1939–to date	Current year only
NORFOLK		
Great Yarmouth Central Library Tolhouse Street Great Yarmouth Norfolk NR30 2SH Tel: 01493 844551 Fax: 01493 857628 Email: yarmouth.lib@norfolk.gov.uk	Current year only	Current year only
PLYMOUTH		
University of Plymouth Library Drake Circus Plymouth PL4 8AA Tel: 01752 232310 Email: libraryservices@plymouth.ac.uk	Current year	1933–69, 1976–to date

Library / Institution	Lloyd's Register	Lloyd's List
SOUTHAMPTON		
Southampton Central Library Civic Centre Southampton S014 7LW Tel: 023 80832205 Email: local.studies@southampton.gov.uk Website: www.southampton.gov.uk	1764, 1768, 1776, 1778–84, 1786–87, 1789–1802, 1804–07, 1809–16, 1818–1900, 1902–05, 1907–69, 1977–85, 1994–95	1741–1826, 1842–50, 1917–18, 1939–45, 1976–93, 1996
Southampton Institute Warsash Campus Newton Road Warsash Southampton S031 9ZL Tel: 023 80319681 Email: library.enquiries@solent.ac.uk	1927–29, 1937–40, 1944–45, 1952–53, 1957–84, 1986–to date	1993–1996
SUNDERLAND		
City Library & Arts Centre 28–30 Fawcett Street Sunderland SR1 1RE Tel: 0191 514 1235 Fax: 0191 514 84444	1816, 1818–22, 1833, 1838, 1848, 1851/52, 1854–58, 1861–63, 1867–69, 1871/72, 1874–to date	Current year only

Bibliography

J. F. Ade Ajayi and Michael Crowder. *The History Of West Africa* (London: Longman, 2 vols. 1971–74)

Edward Braithwaite. *The Development Of Creole Society In Jamaica 1770–1820* (Oxford: Clarendon Press, 1971)

Michael L. Conniff and Thomas Davis. *Africans In The Americas – The History Of Black Diaspora* (New York: St. Martins, 1994)

Isaac Dookhan. *A Post Emancipation History Of West Indies* (London: Collins, 1975)

Guy Grannum. *Tracing Your West Indian Ancestors* (London: PRO Publications, 1995)

Douglas Hall. *In Miserable Slavery, Thomas Thistlewood in Jamaica 1750–1786* (London: Macmillan, 1989)

Richard Hart. *Slaves Who Abolished Slavery: Vol. 1 Blacks in Bondage* (Jamaica: University of West Indies Press, 1980)

Richard Hart. *Slaves Who Abolished Slavery: Blacks in Rebellion* (Jamaica: University of West Indies Press, 1985)

B. W. Higman. *Jamaica Surveyed Plantation Maps And Plans Of The 18th And 19th Centuries* (Kingston, Jamaica: Institute of Jamaica Publications Ltd, 1988)

F. J. Klingberg. *The Anti Slavery Movement in England. A Study in English Humanitarianism* (New Haven: Yale U.P. / London: O.U.P., 1926)

Robin Walker. *Classic Splendour: Roots of Black History* (London: Bogle L'Ouverture Publications Ltd, 1999)

Walter Rodney. *How Europe Underdeveloped Africa* (London: Bogle L'Ouverture, Publications Ltd, 1988)

Ronald Segal. *The Black Diaspora. Five Centuries of the Black Experience Outside Africa* (New York: Farrar, Straus and Giroux, 1995)

Credo Mutwa. *Indaba, My Children, African Tribal History, Legends, Customs and Religious Beliefs* (Edinburgh: Payback Press, 1964)

C.L. Blockson. *Black Genealogy* (Baltimore: Black Classic Press, 1977)

Cornel West. *Race Matters* (Boston: Beacon Press, 1993)

Walton Look Lai. *The Chinese in the West Indies, 1806–1995, A Documented History, the Press* (University of West Indies, 1996)

Eric Williams. *Capitalism and Slavery* (London: André Deutsch, 1964)

Bryan Sykes. *The Seven Daughters of Eve* (New York: WW Norton and Company, 2001)

F. Barham Zincke. *The Days of My Years: A Sequel to Some Materials for the History of Wherstead* (Ipswich: Reed and Barret, 1892)

Acknowledgements

I'd like to thank Daniela de Groote and Gary Pulsifer of Arcadia Books for encouraging me to finally complete this project. I gratefully acknowledge the generous support of the Authors Foundation. Also, I'm extremely grateful to Brother Rema Diallo, a genuinely altruistic human being; without him, I would not have been able to complete my journey. Nor would I be in the privileged position to dedicate this book to: Chief Nene Agbeezee III of Somanya, Ebenezer Kwame Odonkor, Comfort Dede Djaba, Faustina Ayernor, Docia Dede Anyinagmavor, Kosi Woryor, Uncle Kofi Djaba, Brother Clifford Tetteh Dorhetso, Brother Kwadjo and Family and Brother Albie & Sister Rose Walls.

Every effort has been made to trace the copyright holders of all works quoted in this book. Any omission is unintentional, and the publisher would be happy to make due acknowledgement in future editions. Grateful acknowledgement is made to the following:

The National Archives, Kew, Richmond, Surrey, for permission to reproduce:
The Return of Baptisms by Daniel W. Rose (CO/134/144/pg157–162)
The passenger list for the ship *Irpinia*, 1957 (T71/190/pg254)

An extract from the Return of Slaves on the Cousins Cove
   Sugar Plantation, Hanover, Jamaica, 1817 (T71/190/pg254)
   Slave Register Triennial Update – 1826 (T71/193/176)
   Slave Register Triennial Update – 1823 (T71 193 pg175)
The Hyde Park Family Centre, London, for permission to
   reproduce:
   Parish Index – Jamaica 1868
   Parish Index of Baptisms 1800–1836
   Parish Registration – Baptism Record, Jamaica, 1813
The Royal Geographical Society, London, for permission to
   reproduce: Map of Properties – Extract Jamaica West, 1768
The British Library (Newspapers), London, for permission
   to reproduce the advertisement from *The Royal Gazette*,
   Jamaica, Saturday, 19 January 1793
The University of West Indies Press for quotes taken from:
   Slaves Who Abolished Slavery: Blacks in Bondage (1980); and
   Slaves Who Abolished Slavery: Blacks in Rebellion (2002) by
   Richard Hart.
Beacon Press, Boston, for quotes taken from *Race Matters* by
   Cornel West. Copyright © 1993, 2007 Cornel West
Carlton Publishing Group for quotes taken from *Capitalism and
   Slavery* by Eric Williams. Copyright © 1964 Eric Williams
Canongate Books Ltd, Edinburgh, for quotation taken from
   Indaba, My Children by Credo Mutwa

PAUL CROOKS
Ancestors

'A moving tale of a black British family that travels through the ages from slavery and beyond' – Bonnie Greer, *Guardian*

'An inspiring piece of literature. You can also smell the sweat, the blood, hear the cracking whips and bitter cries of a people thrust into bondage' – *The Voice*

HOW A LOST FAMILY WAS FOUND

It is in the late eighteenth century. Aboard a slave ship bound from West Africa to Jamaica, a terrified young boy is cared for by Amy, a fellow captive, who becomes his surrogate mother during that nightmare voyage. They are sold to separate owners, but their lives remain curiously intertwined, and the boy, now a man named August, marries Ami's daughter, Sarah. *Ancestors* tells the story of their lives, their part in the struggle for emancipation, and the hope and faith that sustains them.

At the age of ten, Paul Crook's great-great-great-grandfather John Alexander Crooks was captured and put aboard a slave ship bound for Jamaica. *Ancestors* is the fictionalized account of John's experiences from 1798 to 1838, the year that slaves in the British West Indies were set free.

'An exceptional debut novel. It is rightly being hailed as the heir to Alex Haley's *Roots*... . A highly recommended read for the entire family' – *Woman to Woman*

'Part historical novel, part thriller ... convincingly recreates slave life as it must have been and the helplessness of individual slaves in an unfeeling system'
– *Family History Monthly*

'Crooks' search for his family tree is the compelling theme – fiction based on terrible fact' – *Off the Shelf*